True or False?

Comments and Queries about The New Testament

by Michael Penny

ISBN: 978-1-78364-480-3

www.obt.org.uk

Unless indicated otherwise Scripture quotations are taken from the Holy Bible, New International Version Anglicised Copyright © 1979, 1984, 2011 Biblica. Used by permission of Hodder & Stoughton Ltd, an Hachette UK company. All rights reserved. 'NIV' is a registered trademark of Biblica UK trademark number 1448790.

****

The Open Bible Trust
Fordland Mount, Upper Basildon,
Reading, RG8 8LU, UK.

Contents

Part 5 Comments and Queries about Paul's Later Letters

Publications of The Open Bible Trust must be in accordance with its evangelical, fundamental and dispensational basis. However, beyond this minimum, writers are free to express whatever beliefs they may have as their own understanding, provided that the aim in so doing is to further the object of The Open Bible Trust. A copy of the doctrinal basis is available on **www.obt.org.uk** or from:

THE OPEN BIBLE TRUST
Fordland Mount, Upper Basildon,
Reading, RG8 8LU, GB

Preface: How to use this book

One of the best ways of using this book is to pause after reading the chapter heading, and ask whether or not the statement is 'true or false'. Then, before going on to read what I have to say, stop and consider your view. Do you think the statement is 'true' or do you think it 'false'? And then pause again, to consider the *reasons* why you consider it 'true' or 'false'. After having done so, then please go on to read what I have to say. You may agree with me, you may not.

One reason for publishing this book is to try to get readers to think about and consider the issues raised. Whether or not a reader agrees with me is somewhat secondary. If you read the Open Bible Trust publishing policy on the previous page you will see that, other than the basic doctrines of the Trust, writers are free to express whatever beliefs they may have as their own understanding, providing their aim in doing so is to further the object of the Trust. One of the objects of The Open Bible Trust is to encourage people to open their Bibles and, with an open mind, to consider the views put forward by a speaker or a writer.

My prayer is that readers will find this book not only interesting, but that it will be a stimulus in helping them to think about and consider their own views – not only on the subjects considered here, but also on all subjects within the Christian arena.

Michael Penny

A companion to this book:

True or False?
Comments and Queries about Christianity

See page 183 for details.

Part 1

Comments and Queries about the Gospels

1 Mary and Joseph were not married
True or false?

The general idea that most people have is that one day Joseph learned that there was to be a Roman census which meant he must return to Bethlehem. He and his fiancée duly set off from Nazareth (travelling along with Mary seated on a donkey), arriving late that night in Bethlehem whereupon Jesus was born. I am not sure where this version of the events has its origins; possibly in the mediaeval Mystery Plays. However, the reality would have been very different.

Mystery Plays

Mystery plays are among the earliest formally developed plays in medieval Europe. Medieval mystery plays focused on the representation of Bible stories in churches as tableaux with accompanying antiphonal song. They developed from the 10th to the 16th century, reaching the height of their popularity in the 15th century before being rendered obsolete by the rise of professional theatre.

The plays originated as simple *tropes*, verbal embellishments of liturgical texts, and slowly became more elaborate. As these liturgical dramas increased in popularity, vernacular forms emerged, as travelling companies of actors and theatrical productions organized by local communities became more common in the later Middle Ages.

Nazareth to Bethlehem in a day?

There were two popular routes from Nazareth, south towards Jerusalem and on to Bethlehem. The easier one was through Samaria. However, the Samaritans were not too hospitable to Jews from Galilee *en route* to worship in the temple in Jerusalem. The second involved travelling down the Jordan Valley to Jericho and then up to Jerusalem. This had the advantage of following a source of water, but it had great disadvantage: Jerusalem is 3,000 feet above sea level whereas Jericho is more than 1,000 feet below sea level, and much of this climb would be in the excessively dry air caused by the salt of the Dead Sea drawing moisture out of the atmosphere.

Many years ago the Bible Lands Society produced a well-researched article showing that the most likely route taken by Mary and Joseph would have been through Samaria. It also pointed out that it would have taken ten days to travel from Nazareth to Bethlehem, allowing one Sabbath Day's rest when no travel could take place.

Travel alone?

This was the time of the *Pax Romana*, the Roman Peace. Caesar Augustus was in charge of the Roman Empire, which was experiencing a time of consolidation. It policed its Empire well and there was relative safety for travellers, as Paul experienced on his journeys. However, it was not crime free and our Lord used the illustration of a person falling into the hands of robbers in His parable of the Good Samaritan (Luke 10:30). Thus it is highly unlikely, if not impossible, that Mary and Joseph would have travelled alone. Under normal circumstances there were frequent excursions to Jerusalem from Galilee, and so people travelled in groups, as Mary and Joseph and Jesus did when he was twelve.

> When he was twelve years old, they went up to the Feast, according to the custom. After the Feast was over, while his parents were returning home, the boy Jesus stayed behind in Jerusalem, but they were unaware of it. Thinking he was in their company, they travelled on for a day. Then they began looking for him among their relatives and friends. (Luke 2:42-44)

However, here, as the time of His birth was approaching, we have exceptional circumstances. The Roman decree stated that everyone must return to their own home town. This ensured that there would be more people than usual travelling.

Just Mary and Joseph from the Line of David?

We know that both Mary and Joseph were of the line of David (see the genealogies in Matthew 1:6-7,16; Luke 2:4; 3:23,31). This would have meant that their parents were also of the line of David. Were Joseph's parents living in Galilee? Possibly, but we cannot be certain. But what of Mary's parents? Almost certainly! After spending three months with Elizabeth and Zechariah, John the Baptist was born, and Mary returned *home* to Galilee (Luke 1:26,56), and home for a young virgin pledged to be married would have been with her parents.

At this time the Romans were developing Galilee. It is a lovely area even today, and in those days it seems that rich Romans liked to live or holiday there, and many Roman villas were being built. This may explain why Joseph, a carpenter, left his home town and went north to find work. Bethlehem was poor and there was little work there, and so Joseph may not have been alone and others may well have had to return to Bethlehem to register for the Roman census.

Nine months pregnant?

Would Joseph have undertaken a journey of ten days, on a donkey, when Mary was eight or more months pregnant? It seems highly unlikely. The decree would have been issued with sufficient notice to enable people to make any suitable arrangements for any necessary journeys.

We know that Mary spent about three months with Elizabeth and Zechariah and if, as is possible, it was during her time there that the Holy Spirit came upon her and she conceived, when she got home to Nazareth and broke the news to her parents and Joseph she was probably only about two months pregnant. Joseph's initial reaction was to call off the engagement quietly, but after the angel appeared to him, we read that he "took Mary home as his wife" (Matthew 1:24). What does this mean? Where would 'home' have been for Joseph?

We read in Luke 2:4 that when they left Nazareth Mary was pregnant and they were engaged. These words imply that this verse comes after the time when the angel appeared to Joseph, but before Joseph had taken "Mary home as wife". However, the implication of Matthew 1:24 is that Joseph did so soon after the dream. The question is … where would 'home' have been for Joseph? The natural answer would be Bethlehem, the place to which he was going to register. He was going there not only to register, but also to be with his family … and to get married.

How pregnant would Mary be?

In the first trimester of pregnancy many women feel unwell; during the last trimester they can feel uncomfortably large; in the middle trimester many feel well and seem almost to glow with good health. This may well have been the time when the journey would have been undertaken.

Unmarried when Jesus was born?

The traditional view is that Mary and Joseph were still unmarried when the baby was born. However, if they travelled to his home town when she was about three or four months pregnant they would have had plenty of time to be married – and this is what Matthew tells us happened; Joseph "took Mary home as his wife". Nothing would have been more natural than to go back to one's home town for a family wedding; but is this what happened?

The traditional idea is that they arrived the night the baby was due and, because there was no room in the inn, the baby was born in a stable. However, if we note carefully what Luke 2:6 states, it says *"While they were there*, the time came for the baby to be born". That is, while they were there (in Bethlehem) the time came for the baby to be born. Clearly then, they had been in Bethlehem for some time before the baby was born, and they had had time to get married. If that is the case, why was there no room in the inn?

No room in the inn?

As we have mentioned, both Joseph's line and Mary's line go back through David. Bethlehem was their ancestral home; it seems also to have been their home town. When they returned to Bethlehem, together with Mary's parents and possibly Joseph's, they would have been returning to relatives and it seems that the place where they stayed was an inn. This may have been run by one of the relatives.

Inns in poor towns like Bethlehem were not five star hotels as we know them today, or even like a modern-day motel. Quite often there was one big room. During the day this served as kitchen / dining / sitting room; at night, the beds came out and it served as a dormitory. This would be the normal arrangement and there would be no problem: not, that is, until the baby was born, and then there might have been considerable complication.

Under the Mosaic Law a woman who gave birth to a son would be ceremonially unclean for seven days, and for a daughter it was two weeks (Leviticus 12:2-5). This, in turn, would mean that anyone who had contact with her would also become ceremonially unclean. Thus anyone staying at the inn would become unclean and, if they were *en route* to Jerusalem to worship at the temple, they would not be able to enter the inner courts of the temple and offer sacrifices there until after they had gone through the cleansing rites. This would mean the inn would have to turn away customers, something they probably could not afford to do. What the family may have decided to do was to clean out the stable, put fresh straw in the manger and use that as a crib for the baby.

Conclusion

I do not know if I am correct in every detail here, but the above scenario is more realistic and it does not violate Scripture. However, I cannot see Mary travelling on a donkey over rough terrain for ten days when she was heavily pregnant. Neither can I see them travelling all alone from Nazareth to Bethlehem. It also seems unlikely to me that God would allow His only begotten Son to be born to an unmarried mother; such children carried a heavy stigma in Israel in New Testament times, and clearly the local community saw Him as Joseph's son (Luke 4:22), implying that Joseph was married to Mary when He was born.

2 Parables are earthly stories with heavenly meanings
True or false?

The parables told by our Lord Jesus are lovely stories and appear (deceptively) easy to understand. They have been described as 'earthly stories with heavenly meanings', but do they, in fact, make His teachings clearer? Some would say so, but there was one significant group of people who would not have agreed that parables made Christ's teaching easier to understand, namely, the Twelve Disciples.

Our Lord did not use parables during the first years of His ministry. It is not until we get to Matthew 13 that we encounter the first parable, and the reaction of the disciples can be summed up in two verses.

> Matthew 13:10: The disciples came to him and asked, "Why do you speak to the people in parables?"

> Matthew 13:36: His disciples came to him and said, "Explain to us the parable of the weeds in the field."

Here the disciples were intrigued as to why Christ started to teach the people in parables. Our Lord's answer was:

> "Though seeing, they do not see; though hearing, they do not hear or understand." (Matthew 13:13)

In other words, they would understand something by the parable, but they would not see the real meaning.

Parabole

The Greek word for 'parable' is *parabole* and it denotes "a placing beside, to lay beside, to compare" (Vine's *Expository Dictionary of New Testament Words*), rather like the word 'parallel' in some ways. It signifies a placing of one thing beside another with a view to comparison. We would naturally expect this to be done in such a way that the comparison would make the original clearer and easier to understand, but this need not be the case. The second may be laid beside the first, but placed in front of it, so as to obscure the first and make it less clear. That seems to be the case with parables. As Christ said, they would be seeing, but they would not see; they would hear, but they would not understand. If this was the case, how did Christ conceal His teaching?

Exaggeration

We normally use the word 'hyperbole' to describe an extreme exaggeration. In mathematics the curve known as the 'hyperbola' goes off to infinity, but so, too, does the curve known as a 'parabola'. Thus it seems that parables contain extreme exaggerations which would grab the attention of those genuinely interested in what Christ taught, but would be to the amusement of the casual listener who would focus on the impossibility of what had been said, and so be blinded as to the true, underlying meaning.

Examples

We might, for example, read the parable of the sower and see nothing unusual in it. However, it has a mighty punch line: the good seed produced a crop of "a hundred[1], sixty or thirty times what was sown" (Matthew 13:8,23). As soon as Christ said this it is likely that many of his listeners would have been startled; they may have shaken their heads in unbelief, or simply laughed. Why? Because the average yield in Palestine at that time would have been about seven times; ten times

---

[1] We read in Genesis 26:12 that "Isaac planted crops in that land and the same year reaped a hundred fold." However, it goes on to explain that the reason this happened was that "the Lord was with him". Any of Christ's listeners who recalled this episode in Genesis would possibly have recognised that the kingdom of heaven would not come unless there was action from God.

would have been a bumper harvest. What Christ said was nonsense, a joke, an exaggeration. It was impossible.

The parable of the weeds (Matthew 13:24-30) would have been received with equal incredulity. No farmer, especially not in Palestine at that time with its limited rain fall and shortage of water, would have left the weeds to grow with the wheat. The former would have robbed the wheat of much needed moisture and would have ensured a poorer yield. Once again, what Christ said would have been greeted with disbelief.

Yeast was a standard symbol for sin throughout the Old Testament [2], so how could Jesus use 'yeast' of the kingdom of heaven? (Matthew 13:33). Such an analogy would have perplexed those who heard Him!

And in the real world of His day (and even now) would anyone truly have sold every single thing they possessed to buy one pearl? (Matthew 13:45-46). Where would they get their money to buy food or pay the rent?

And as for the man who found a treasure in another's field (Matthew 13:44), would it not have been dishonest to have bought that field for a price lower than its real value and, especially, to have concealed the presence of the treasure from the owner of that field (and hence the true owner of the treasure)?

It seems, then, that the parables that Jesus told had an exaggerated or unlikely twist in them; a twist which might bemuse or bewilder, perplex or puzzle, or even humour His listeners, but one which would keep the casual listener from looking for the underlying meaning.

> Two dangers are to be avoided in seeking to interpret the parables in Scripture, that of ignoring the important features, and that of trying to make all the details mean something.
> (W E Vine, *Expository Dictionary of New Testament Words*)

---

[2] And everywhere in the New Testament, except here.

Finding the exaggeration[3]

It may not always be easy for us to find the exaggeration in the parable, possibly because we are not familiar with the conditions and customs of that time. However, it is one of the important features and it is a beneficial exercise for us to look for them. Clearly, in the parable of *The Good Samaritan* the 'Samaritan' is the exaggeration (Luke 10:25-37). After ridiculing the priest and the Levite His listeners would have expected someone like a tax collector to be the hero, certainly not a Samaritan! Jews did not associate with Samaritans and Samaritans did not help Jews who were on their way to Jerusalem to worship at the temple (John 4:9; Luke 9:52-53). Nonetheless, Christ used a Samaritan as the model to follow, and those listening who opposed Christ may well have scoffed and missed the lesson.

And in the parable of the Lost Sheep, no good shepherd would leave ninety-nine unguarded while he went off to look for one stray (Luke 15:4-5). In the real world of Christ's time on earth, this would not have happened. Again, those who were unsympathetic to the Lord may well have been amused by such an improbable situation. Thus we can see that some listening, seeing would not see and hearing would not understand (Matthew 13:13).

When we discover the exaggeration in a parable, let us not be simply bemused or amused by it. Let us use

> **Matthew 18:21-35:**
> **The Unmerciful Servant**.
>
> In 4 BC the whole of Galilee and Perea paid taxes to the Romans of only 200 talents. Verse 24 states he owed ten thousand talents. What an exaggeration!
>
> But 10,000 talents = 100,000,000 denarii
> Contrast the 100 denarii owed *to* the servant with 100,000,000 owed *by* the servant. Another great exaggeration!

---

[3] For more on parables, listen to the Bible Study CDs *A Systematic Approach to Parables* by Michael Penny published by The Open Bible Trust and available from its website (www.obt.org.uk). Also his book *The Purpose of Parables*.

it to explore and appreciate the fuller and deeper meaning in what our Lord has taught. For example, in the parables of the kingdom in Matthew 13, His general message is quite simply to show that when the Kingdom of Heaven is set up on this earth, it will be nothing like any kingdom that has ever been seen before. It will be completely different. Quite simply, it will be amazing ... unbelievable!

3 Ideally, we should sell all we have and give to the poor
True or false?

A little while ago I attended a series of inter-denominational Lent Studies. They were based on the Gospel of Mark and we had some good debate, discussing how the various selected passages applied to Christians. However, one week the passage before us was Mark 10:17-22:

> As Jesus started on his way, a man ran up to him and fell on his knees before him. "Good teacher," he asked, "what must I do to inherit eternal life?" "Why do you call me good?" Jesus answered. "No-one is good - except God alone. You know the commandments: 'Do not murder, do not commit adultery, do not steal, do not give false testimony, do not defraud, honour your father and mother.'" "Teacher," he declared, "all these I have kept since I was a boy." Jesus looked at him and loved him. "One thing you lack," he said. "Go, sell everything you have and give to the poor, and you will have treasure in heaven. Then come, follow me." At this the man's face fell. He went away sad, because he had great wealth.

There was some uneasiness, and the discussion was floundering. People were clearly having problems applying these verses to themselves. I then suggested that perhaps it was injudicious for us to think that we should be able to apply this episode to ourselves. After all, these words had been addressed to only one individual, and the Lord knew him, and his position and problems. This is the only person recorded in Scripture that the Lord told to "sell *all* you have and give to the poor", so, I asked, were we right to think we should do the same?

One lady's eyes lit up! She remarked that she had never thought about this principle before, and she could think of a number of one-off incidents in the Bible that she had difficulty in applying to herself. However, her enthusiasm was soon squashed when her minister, who was part of our group, jumped in. He stated that we couldn't pick and choose what we liked, and stated emphatically that all the Bible is relevant and applicable to us. But is it? It is definitely profitable, but is it all applicable, even the New Testament?

How many of us sacrifice animals? How many of us do not light fires on the Sabbath? How many of us sell all we have and give it to the poor? How many of us live in Christian groups which share everything and have all things in common?

The minister went on to say that we needed to take the passage literally, but look for the generality, and that it was teaching us that we should be generous in our giving. I cannot disagree with the latter sentiment, but that is simply not what Mark 10:17-22 is saying. If we want to encourage giving, then let us go to the clear doctrinal passages of Scripture which deal with that subject in general (e.g. Acts 20:35; 2 Corinthians 9:7; 1 Timothy 6:17-18).

Give all!

When writing to Timothy on this subject, Paul did not draw on these verses from Mark. He did not encourage the rich to give *all* they had. Rather he wrote:

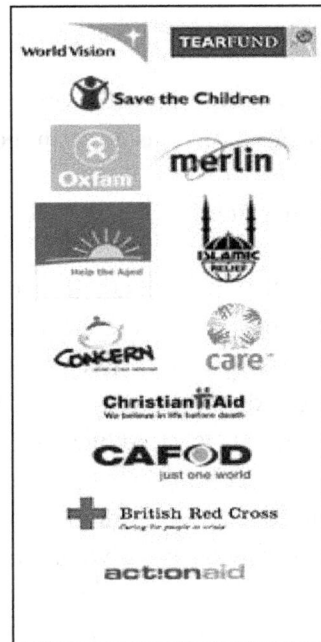

> Command those who are rich in this present world not to be arrogant nor to put their hope in wealth, which is so uncertain, but to put their hope in God, who richly provides us with everything for our enjoyment. Command them to do good, to be rich in good deeds, and to be generous and willing to share. In this way they will lay up treasure for themselves as a firm foundation for the coming age, so that they may take hold of the life that is truly life. (1 Timothy 6:17-19)

This, surely, is much more appropriate advice for us to follow.

Give half!

The idea of building teaching for today on individual, personal cases in the Bible, rather than on doctrinal passages, is that we can find differing situations. Instead of selling everything, we could tell people to follow the example of Zacchaeus, who, when he met Jesus said, "Look, Lord! Here and now I give *half* of my possessions to the poor." Paul did not advise the Corinthians to "give half", but told them to "give according to their means" (2 Corinthians 8:10-13). And he touched on this subject again, a little later.

> Remember this: Whoever sows sparingly will also reap sparingly, and whoever sows generously will also reap generously. Each man should give what he has decided in his heart to give, not reluctantly or under compulsion, for God loves a cheerful giver. (2 Corinthians 9:6-7)

Again, this is much more appropriate for us. Let us give according to our means and let us do so, not dutifully, but cheerfully.

Sell a field!

Another individual, Barnabas, "sold a field he owned and brought the money and put it at the apostles' feet" (Acts 4:37). However, Paul did not advise the Ephesian elders to sell their capital assets; instead he reminded them of the Lord's words: but *not* the words to "sell all you have" but rather "It is more blessed [happy] to give than to receive" (Acts 20:35). This was how he encouraged them to work hard in order to help the weak and poor. As children we may derive greater happiness from receiving, rather than by giving. As new Christians we may experience great comfort from the blessings we receive from the Lord – e.g. forgiveness and eternal life. However, a test of Christian maturity is that we gain greater happiness and contentment from giving and sharing rather than from either receiving from others or keeping what we have to ourselves.

4 Peter is the Rock
True or false?

Matthew 16:13-18

When Jesus came to the region of Caesarea Philippi, he asked his disciples, "Who do people say the Son of Man is?" They replied, "Some say John the Baptist; others say Elijah; and still others, Jeremiah or one of the prophets."

"But what about you?" he asked. "Who do you say I am?"

Simon Peter answered, "You are the Christ, the Son of the living God."

Jesus replied, "Blessed are you, Simon son of Jonah, for this was not revealed to you by man, but by my Father in heaven. And I tell you that you are Peter, and on this rock I will build my church, and the gates of Hades will not overcome it."

In Matthew's Gospel we read of our Lord Jesus Christ saying to Peter, "I tell you that you are Peter, and on this rock I will build my church." This has led some people to the view that Peter is the rock on which Christ's church is built, but is this the case?

Peter, like us all, is a frail human being, a sinner, and within minutes, if not seconds, of making this statement, the Lord turns to Peter and reprimands him with the words, "Get behind me, Satan! You are a stumbling block to me; you do not have in mind the things of God, but the things of men." (Matthew 16:23). Hardly a fitting comment for a person who, according to some, is the rock on which Christ's church is built.

I find Peter a wonderful man. The Bible is not slow to bring before us the weaknesses, failings and sins of its leading characters. We have David and Bathsheba. We have Paul and Barnabas disagreeing so strongly that they go their separate ways. And then there is Peter, who denied the Lord three times, and who caused many in Antioch to stumble because he refused to eat with the Gentiles (Galatians 2:11-21). I think we all, at times, can be like that; on the spur of the moment, or under pressure, we can easily say and do the wrong thing. However, when Peter had time to think things through, he always came to the right conclusion and did the right thing, as he did a little while after the Antioch incident in which he totally supported Paul at the Jerusalem Council (Acts 15:7-11).

Thus I can identify with Peter[4] and find in him great comfort and motivation; but is he the rock on which Christ's church is built?

Rocks and Stones

Augustus Toplady wrote the beautiful hymn *Rock of Ages* but, in that hymn, the rock is not Peter but another person, the Lord Jesus Christ. I think Toplady must be correct in this, for if we search the Bible there are many references to 'the rock'. Consider for example: 1 Corinthians 10:3-4: "They all ate the same spiritual food and drank the same spiritual drink; for they drank from the spiritual rock that accompanied them, and that rock was Christ."

In Romans 9:33 Paul makes it clear that the rock and the stone is none other than the Lord Jesus Christ; He is the One in whom we trust: "See, I lay in Zion a stone that causes men to stumble and a rock that makes them fall, and the one who trusts in him will never be put to shame."

And Peter makes it abundantly clear that the stone is the Lord Jesus Christ: "As you come to him, the living Stone - rejected by men but chosen by God and precious to him" (1 Peter 2:4).

And in the Old Testament, Peter's Scriptures, we read:

> The Lord is my *rock*, and my fortress and my deliverer; my God, my *rock*, in whom I take refuge. (Psalm 18:2, ESV)

---

[4] For more on Peter see *Peter: His life and letters* by Michael Penny, published by The Open Bible Trust.

For who is God besides the LORD? And who is the *Rock* except our God? (Psalm 18:31)

The LORD lives! Praise be to my *Rock*! Exalted be God my Saviour! (Psalm 18:46)

Peter would not have seen himself as 'the rock'

Foundations and Corner Stones

In those days it was considered prudent to make the foundation of the house a rock, and so people built their houses upon rock where possible. Writing to the Corinthians Paul said, "By the grace God has given me, I laid a foundation as an expert builder, and someone else is building on it. But each one should be careful how he builds. For no one can lay any foundation other than the one already laid, which is Jesus Christ" (1 Corinthians 3:10-11).

When there was no rock available to build on, a foundation stone (or corner stone) would be required; all measurements would be taken from that stone and others built on it and around it. Paul refers to this in Ephesians 2:19-20: "Consequently, you are no longer foreigners and aliens, but fellow-citizens with God's people and members of God's household, built on the foundation of the apostles and prophets, with Christ Jesus himself as the chief cornerstone."

But note, in this verse, Paul is *not* saying that the apostles and prophets are the foundation. He has already written that there is no other foundation than Jesus Christ. In Ephesians 2:19-20 he informs the Gentiles that they have the same foundation as the apostles and prophets, namely Jesus Christ, who is the chief cornerstone of that foundation.

Peter uses the same allusion in 1 Peter 2:6: "See, I lay a stone in Zion, a chosen and precious cornerstone, and the one who trusts in him will never be put to shame."

The Corner Stone and Capstone

If the corner stone was the first stone laid, then the capstone was the last. It was the final stone laid on the roof, often a heavy stone to keep those below it firmly in place. "The stone the builders rejected has become the capstone" (Matthew 21:42; see also 1 Peter 2:7). Thus Christ is the cornerstone and capstone; He is the first stone and the last stone; He is the first and last, the Alpha and the Omega.

Two words and two people

Some see Peter's statement "You are the Christ, the Son of the living God" as the 'rock' to which Christ refers. However, it is more likely that Christ has made a play on two words and is contrasting two people.

The Greek for 'Peter' is *petros* and 'rock' is *petra*. According to Vine's *Expository Dictionary of New Testament Words*, *petros* is "a detached stone or boulder, or a stone that might be thrown or easily moved". *Petra*, on the other hand, like the spectacular city of Petra in Jordan, "denotes a mass of rock". Thus as I picture the conversation, I see Christ pointing to Peter and saying, "You are a little stone" and then, pointing to Himself, He says, "and upon this solid rock will I build my church."

5 People need faith to be healed
True or false?

It is understandable that people with debilitating illnesses and conditions have a great desire to be healed. However, it is even more understandable if those people live in a country which does not have a health care service. There are many Americans who eagerly follow Christian faith healers, and when one realises that a significant proportion of the population in that country has no health care, or have inadequate health care, one begins to realise why such 'faith healers' gain a following.

Even though such 'faith healers' may have a modicum of success in healing in some areas such as back aches and depression, the results for more serious conditions are poor. However, they do not take the failure upon themselves or rethink their theology. Rather they blame the invalid, often stating that the sick person does not have the 'faith to be healed'. However, in New Testament times, was it necessary to have faith to be healed?

From most English translations it looks as if it does. Consider, for example, the account of the healing of the ten lepers (Luke 17:12-19). Our Lord healed all these men, but only one returned and threw himself at Jesus' feet and thanked Him. Christ's reply to that man was, "Rise and go; your faith has made you well." However, the other nine were healed also! So where was their faith?

Three words translated 'heal'.

Greek has three different words which have been translated 'heal' in the New Testament[5].

1. *Therapeuo*: this gives us the word 'therapeutic' and occurs 44 times. It is always translated heal or cure, except in Acts 17:25

---

[5] For more on these words and the significance of healing in the New Testament see chapter 11 of *The Miracles of the Apostles* by Michael Penny (OBT).

where it is rendered 'worship' in the *KJV* and 'served' in the *NIV*. It **never** occurs in such phrases as 'your faith has healed you'.

2. *Iaomai* and its derivatives occur 34 times and it is always translated 'heal' or 'made whole'. However, it, also, **never** occurs in such phrases as "your faith has healed you" or "your faith has made you well'.

3. *Sozo:* this is the third word which, in a few of its references, is translated 'heal' but mostly it is the word for 'save' and it occurs in such passages as Romans 10:9 where we read, "If you confess with your mouth, 'Jesus is Lord,' and **believe** in your heart that God raised him from the dead, you will be **saved**." In other words, this is the 'salvation' word and we know that it is by grace that we have been **saved**, through **faith** (Ephesians 2:8).

Faith and salvation

As we study the New Testament we find the word *pistis* (translated 'faith', 'believe' or 'trust') is intimately linked with the word *sozo* (translated 'saved'). Thus whenever the two are in close proximity, the translation of *sozo* should be 'saved'. This would make eminent sense in the case of the one leper who returned. All ten were 'healed' by Christ's power. One returned, fell down at his feet, worshipped Him and thanked Him. To him Christ said "Rise up and go; your faith has **saved** you." Thus the man did not need faith to be healed, but he definitely needed faith to be saved.

It is the same with blind Bartimaeus (Mark 10:46-52). Most English versions conclude this section with Christ's statement "your faith has healed you", but just think of the number of people our Lord healed who did not have faith; e.g. the blind and dumb demon-possessed man we read of in Matthew 12:22.

However, in Mark 10:52 Young's *Literal Translation of the Bible* has "Go, thy faith hath saved thee." In this, Young must be correct. Earlier

Bartimeaus had not just called out "Jesus! ... Jesus!" He had shouted "Jesus! Son of David!" Bartimaeus believed Jesus was the Son of David, the Messiah, the Christ, and for that he was 'saved' (John 20:31).

We have exactly the same expression in Luke 7:50, but here the translators have "Your faith has saved you; go in peace." If the translators had been consistent they would have translated all the other passages which link *pistis* and *sozo* the same.

Again we have the same expression in Luke 18:42. Here the *NIV* translates it as "Your faith has healed you," but the *KJV* has "Thy faith hath saved thee".

The Gentile Cripple in Lystra

In Acts 14:8-10 we have the account of Paul preaching in Lystra. We read of a crippled man who listened to Paul, and we read that Paul "saw that he had faith to be *healed*" and he healed him. Was Paul preaching a healing message? Or was he proclaiming Christ and the salvation that comes through faith in Him?

We have a number of Paul's speeches recorded in Acts and in none of these is there a healing message. Rather each one exalts the Lord Jesus Christ. It is doubtful if this pagan man knew anything about Paul's ability to heal. Rather he was listening to what Paul said about Jesus Christ, and he believed what Paul said. Thus Paul looked on him and saw "he had faith to be *saved*." Seeing such a pagan putting his trust in Christ, moved Paul and he felt compassion for the man and healed him. I suggest that this is a more credible scenario and one which is in harmony with the overall teaching of the New Testament that faith is required for salvation, not for healing.

A woman with an issue of blood

The well-known account of the woman touching the hem of Christ's garment ends with our Lord saying to her, "Your faith has *healed* you.

Go in peace." (Luke 8:48). However, it was **not** her faith which 'healed' her; it was touching the hem of Christ's cloak which healed her.

Who did she think Jesus was that just by touching his cloak she would be healed? Did she, like Bartimaeus, believe Him to be the Messiah?

She was, however, scared, but Christ looked at her, calmed her, and told her that her faith had 'saved' her. She was forgiven and she had eternal life and thus she could "Go in peace." Being physically healthy does not necessarily bring 'peace,' but believing that we are loved by God, forgiven by Him, and have eternal life most certainly does.

6 The Kingdom of God is within you
True or false?

Once, having been asked by the Pharisees when the kingdom of God would come, Jesus replied, "The kingdom of God does not come with your careful observation, nor will people say, 'Here it is,' or 'There it is,' because the kingdom of God is *within* you" (Luke 17:20-21).

The Problem

To many there is no problem with this well-known verse, for they see the kingdom of God as being Christ's rule in the hearts of all believers. However, this cannot be the correct understanding of this verse.

> An inner condition of the soul may qualify for admission to the kingdom, but it is not itself the kingdom. (J. M. Creed, *The Gospel According to St. Luke*)

> Jesus speaks elsewhere of men entering the kingdom, not of the kingdom entering men. The kingdom is a state of affairs, not a state of mind. (T. W. Manson, *The Mission and Message of Jesus*)

When?

In no way do I wish to detract from the blessed truths of Christ living in our hearts by faith (Ephesians 3:17) and of all believers being sealed with the Holy Spirit as a permanent possession (Ephesians 1:13-14). Neither of these facts was true when our Lord spoke those words. He was on earth and the Spirit had not yet been given. Thus we must avoid one of the common errors leading to a misunderstanding of passages in the Bible: that of reading teaching for a later time back into an earlier time, back into a time when that teaching simply could not have been true. In trying to understand this passage we must keep to the teaching of the Gospels.

Who?

The problem is exacerbated when we consider to **whom** this comment was addressed. It was to the Pharisees, unbelievers, the Lord's greatest opponents. They did not believe in Him so how could the kingdom of God be within them? In fact Matthew 23:13 states, "Woe to you, teachers of the law and Pharisees, you hypocrites! You shut the kingdom of heaven in men's faces. You yourselves do not enter, nor will you let those enter who are trying to." Thus the Pharisees had **nothing** to do with the kingdom.

Where?

This conversation took place in Israel, and the word "you" is plural. Thus some commentators take our Lord's words to refer not to the Pharisees, but to Israel at large. Their view is that "the Kingdom of God, through its efficacy and power brought by Him [the Saviour] on earth, is already within the circle of Jewry" (Norval Geldenhuys, *Commentary on the Gospel of Luke*).

There are also examples in Greek where the preposition *entos* (within), when used with the plural "you", can be translated "among". This would render the expression "The kingdom of God is among you". In this case, the Saviour declares that the kingdom has arrived and is *among the Jews* because He, Himself, is there as the representative of the kingdom (see T. W. Manson).

However, our Lord's own words in Luke 17:21 show that such explanations are deficient.

What?

The Pharisees wanted to know when the Kingdom of God would come. Our Lord's answer was that "The kingdom of God does not come from careful observation" (Luke 17:20). Vine, in his *Expository Dictionary of New Testament Words*, defines "careful observation" as "attentive watching". What does the Lord mean by this? He expands this by saying,

"Nor will people say, 'Here it is,' or 'There it is'" (Luke 17:21). But what do those expressions mean? Fortunately we have similar expressions in the context, and elsewhere in Scripture, relating to His second coming.

In Luke 17:22-24, we read that our Lord said to His disciples, "The time is coming when you will long to see one of the days of the Son of Man, but you will not see it. Men will tell you, 'There he is!' or 'Here he is!' Do not go running off after them. For the Son of Man in his day will be like the lightning, which flashes and lights up the sky from one end to the other."

In Matthew 24:23 we read, "At that time if anyone says to you, 'Look, here is the Christ!' or, 'There he is!' do not believe it."

And in Matthew 24:26-27, "So if anyone tells you, 'There he is, out in the desert,' do not go out; or, 'Here he is, in the inner rooms,' do not believe it. For as lightning that comes from the east is visible even in the west, so will be the coming of the Son of Man."

In other words, if the people in Israel are *wondering* about when the Son of Man will return and say that He has returned, and that you can prove it by looking for Him in this place or in that place, then clearly they are wrong. If they have to watch carefully and pay careful attention to details to see whether or not Christ has returned, then those who say He has returned are wrong!

When the Son of Man returns it will be as clear as lightning in the sky. It will be seen by all in Israel and will be known by all in Israel. Similarly when the kingdom of God comes, it will be seen by all in Israel and will be known by all in Israel. Discussing whether the kingdom was, at that time, within the Pharisees or within Israel, or whether it was among them because Christ was among them ... each one of these is a case of "Here it is" or "There it is", and so such explanations are erroneous. That being the case, what did our Lord mean by "The kingdom of God is *within* you?"

Many modern archaeological discoveries have validated the historical accuracy of the Bible and have helped Bible scholars understand the meaning of certain ancient words ... In Koine Greek, the expression *entos humon* (literally, 'inside of you') often meant 'within reach'. Thus Jesus' statement in Luke 17:21 could mean 'The kingdom is *within reach.*' (Philip W Comfort, p 273 *The Origin of the Bible*).

This makes excellent sense. We know that both John the Baptist and our Lord Jesus started off their ministries with the words, "The kingdom of heaven is near" (Matthew 3:1,17). We also know that our Saviour made a number of statements such as:

Matthew 10:23: "When you are persecuted in one place, flee to another. I tell you the truth, you will not finish going through the cities of Israel *before* the Son of Man comes."

Matthew 16:28: "I tell you the truth, some who are standing here will not taste death *before* they see the Son of Man coming in his kingdom."

Such statements as these make it clear that the kingdom was intimately associated with the second coming of Christ. They also show that the kingdom and the second coming were *possible* imminent events; they were "within reach"; they could have come about within the lifetime of that generation (see Matthew 24:34).

Why *possible*?

I say "possible" because, as the English translation stands, it looks as if our Saviour made rather definite statements which turned out to be incorrect, as His return and the kingdom did not happen at that time. However, the word "before" in each of these passages is the Greek *eos an*, and the particle *an* is "peculiar to Greek, incapable of translation by a single word; it denotes that the action of the verb is dependent on some circumstance or action" (Walter Bauer, *A Greek-English Lexicon of the New Testament and other Early Christian Literature*).

Note that: it is *dependent* upon some circumstance or action. Thus what our Lord said was, "*It is possible* that some who are standing here will not taste death before they see the Son of Man coming in his kingdom". It was possible. It was within reach. It depended. It depended on "some circumstance ... or action". That "circumstance or action" is outlined for us in Acts 3:19-21. There Peter, speaking to the people of Israel, said,

> "Repent, then, and turn to God, so that your sins may be wiped out, that times of refreshing may come from the Lord, and that *he may send the Christ*, who has been appointed for you - even Jesus. *He must remain in heaven until* the time comes for God to restore everything, as he promised long ago through his holy prophets."

If the people of Israel repented, if they turned to God, not only would their sins be wiped out, but Christ would return from heaven and the kingdom would be set up. Would this happen at that time? That was what the disciples wanted to know in Acts 1:6 when they asked, "Are you, *at this time* going to restore the kingdom to Israel?"

So the key to the kingdom coming was the repentance of the people of Israel, including the Pharisees, who, like the disciples in Acts 1:6, also wanted to know "when the kingdom of God would come" (Luke 17:20). The Lord Jesus Christ told them, "The kingdom of God is *within reach*". All they needed to do was to repent, rather than to rest in their self-righteousness. They needed to turn to God rather than remain in their traditions. If they repented and turned to God, then many others would also do so, but did they?

We know from history that neither the majority of the Pharisees, nor the majority of the people of Israel, repented and turned to God. The generation to whom Jesus spoke rejected and crucified Him. The Jews of the Acts period beat, imprisoned, and stoned the apostles, and so the necessary "circumstance or action" did not come about. The kingdom may have been "near" when John the Baptist and our Lord ministered. It may have been "within reach" of those people alive at that time. It could have happened before that generation passed away, but their hardness of heart, their blindness and their deafness, rendered the people of Israel useless (Acts 28:25-27). Christ's coming and the kingdom upon this earth were postponed, so to speak, until a future day. At the end of the Acts period God's salvation was sent to the Gentiles (Acts 28:28), and a new dispensation of grace commenced. What had once been "within reach" was now "beyond their grasp".

Application

No one has yet been able to clearly ascertain what the balance is between the sovereignty of God and the responsibility of man. Clearly, at that time, God had chosen to make the return of Christ and the setting up of the kingdom on earth dependent upon the repentance of Israel and their acceptance of Christ.

One view is that man's actions may delay God's plans, but never thwart them. What we have been considering here may be just one such example. However, Christ will most definitely come back one day and will set up His kingdom upon this earth; but whether that will be in our life-time or not is a moot point. The fact remains that people today can still have a Pharisaic attitude: one of self-righteousness, with religious traditions and rituals being more important than faith in Christ Himself. For us the kingdom on earth may not be *within reach*, but eternal life is. Let us bow the knee at the Cross of Christ, admitting that we are sinners and looking to Him for forgiveness.[6]

---

[6] If you like the approach used in this chapter (i.e. systematically going through Who? ... When? ... Where? .... What? ... Why? ... before seeking an Application) you may care to read *40 Problem Passages* by Michael Penny which tackles some difficult passages using this approach.

7 You must ask 'in My name' to receive answers to prayer
True or false?

Three times in John's Gospel we read of our Lord Jesus Christ telling His disciples that they would be given whatever they asked for, provided they asked *in His name*. The following are the precise words our Saviour spoke.

> "And *I will do whatever you ask in my name*, so that the Son may bring glory to the Father. *You may ask me for anything in my name, and I will do it*." (John 14:13-14)

> "You did not choose me, but I chose you and appointed you to go and bear fruit - fruit that will last. Then *the Father will give you whatever you ask in my name*." (John 15:16)

> "In that day you will no longer ask me anything. I tell you the truth, *my Father will give you whatever you ask in my name*. Until now you have not asked for anything in my name. *Ask and you will receive*, and your joy will be complete. Though I have been speaking figuratively, a time is coming when I will no longer use this kind of language but will tell you plainly about my Father. In that day *you will ask in my name*. I am not saying that I will ask the Father on your behalf." (John 16:23-26)

The right 'form of words'

Now many great saints have found that, although they have asked, they have not received. This has led them to seek the right *form of words* with which to **end** their prayers. If we consider some of the well-established prayers we will see that they often **end** with expressions that mention our Lord Jesus Christ. Consider, for example, the four prayers below.

A prayer of Saint Augustine	The Master Carpenter Prayer
Eternal God, who art the light of the minds that know thee, the joy of the hearts that love thee, and the strength of the wills that serve thee: Grant us so to know thee that we may truly love thee, and so to love thee that we may fully serve thee, whom to serve is perfect freedom, *in Jesus Christ our Lord.*	Jesus, Master Carpenter of Bethlehem, who on the cross through wood and nails didst work man's whole salvation: Wield well thy tools in this thy workshop; that we who come to thee roughly hewn may, by thy hand be fashioned to a truer beauty and a greater usefulness, *for the honour of Thy name.*
Collect from the Leonine Sacramentary	Vesper Collect
Remember, O Lord, what thou hast wrought in us, and not what we deserve; and as thou has called us to thy service, make us worthy of our calling; *through Jesus Christ our Lord.*	Lighten our darkness, we beseech thee, O Lord, and by thy great mercy defend us from all perils and dangers of this night, *for the love of thy only Son, our Saviour Jesus Christ.*

When we consider these we see each has a different form of words with which the prayers end. They are:

- in Jesus Christ our Lord;
- through Jesus Christ our Lord;
- for the honour of Thy name;
- for the love of thy only Son, our Saviour Jesus Christ.

And if we consider more prayers, we will see an even greater variety of endings.

- Through Christ our Lord; *The Collect for Purity.*
- Through Him who liveth and reigneth with thee and the Holy Ghost, now and for ever; *The Advent Collect.*
- Through the same our Lord Jesus Christ, who liveth and reigneth with thee and the same Spirit, ever one God, world without end; *The Collect for the Nativity.*
- Through Jesus Christ our Lord, who liveth and reigneth with thee and the Holy Ghost, ever one God, world without end; *The Easter Collect.*
- Through the merits of Christ Jesus our Saviour, who liveth and reigneth with thee, in the unity of the same Spirit, one God, world without end; *The Whitsun Collect*
- Through Jesus Christ our Lord, to whom with thee and the Holy Ghost be all honour and glory, world without end; *The General Thanksgiving.*

Now some of these are rather lengthy and, to some minds, rather *flowery*, but there is nothing wrong with any of them for they all seek to glorify, exalt and magnify our heavenly Father and the Holy Spirit, as well as our Saviour. However, some in evangelical circles object to all the endings mentioned above. They insist that the only way to end a prayer, to ensure that it is answered, is with the correct *form of words* which is, basically, "… and this we ask in the name of Jesus Christ our Lord".

Yet does this so called 'correct' form of words, or indeed any other form of words, guarantee that we will receive what we ask for? If we are honest, we shall have to answer that question with a resounding "No!", and this should not surprise us, for how can God 'rubber stamp' anything and everything we ask for, just because we use the right form of words? That would not be prayer; that would be like a Harry Potter magic spell![7]

---

[7] For more on why prayer is not answered see *Unanswered Prayer* by Neville Stephens, *The Place of Prayer in an Age of Grace* by Michael Penny and numbers 19 & 20 in *40 Problem Passages* by Michael Penny. There are also a number of Bible Study CDs on the OBT website (www.obt.org.uk) which deal with this issue.

In the name of Jesus

It is interesting to note that there is not one prayer in the Scriptures which ends with the words "in the name of Jesus" or "in His name" or "in the name of our Lord Jesus Christ", or even any similar ending. In fact the prayers of Scripture have a wide variety of endings, which might suggest that the words with which we **end** our prayers can have nothing to do with asking in Christ's name.

The meaning of to "to ask in the name of Christ" is best viewed as an ambassadorial expression. In other words, when we pray we should view ourselves as Christ's ambassadors upon this earth. The American ambassador to Britain can say only what the US administration tells him he can say; he can follow only the President's policies and say what the President would say if he had been able to be there. Similarly, Christians should say only what Christ would say if He were in our place. We should say only what is in line with His revealed will. As Metropolitan Anthony puts it in *Jesus: Then and Now*:

> Do you think that when God says 'No' to our prayers, we are tempted to think that is not an answer? Yes; it happens [that we get 'No'] because very primitive people who claim to be believers imagine that because they have ended their prayer by saying, 'And this we ask in Jesus Christ's name', the answer must be 'Yes'. But it is not so simple. To ask in Christ's name means to ask with the intention that my prayers should be that of Christ if he were here in my place. It is not a way of forcing God's hand. When Christ says, 'Whatever you ask in my name, it shall be done to you', it does not mean we can force his hand by saying, 'It is in Christ's name that I will do it, and therefore you must'. It means that from within my oneness with Christ these are the words I speak. If there is no oneness in Christ in what you ask, then you are not speaking in Christ's name. I think that any Christian's prayers should be such that Christ could have said it in our place.

Rushing into prayer, and ending it with the words "and this we ask in the name of Jesus" is most definitely **not** asking "in His name". If we want to pray "in His name", rather than worrying about the ending we need to stop and think ... even before we *begin* to pray. If we are going to approach the throne of grace 'in Christ's name' then we need to stop and ask ourselves, just what would our Lord Jesus pray for if He were here now? If He were here, in my place, what would He say? If we ask such questions, we may find that we do not know all the answers and that will stop us rushing into prayer. And if we do know the answers, we might find that either we modify our prayer significantly or we do not even begin to pray for what we were going to pray.

8 The day we die we enter paradise True or false?

As many know, our Lord Jesus Christ was crucified between criminals. One of them hurled insults at him, but was rebuked by the other, who said to him, "Don't you fear God?" and went on to say, "We are punished justly, for we are getting what our deeds deserve. But this man has done nothing wrong." Then he turned to our Lord and said, "Jesus, remember me when you come into your kingdom." To which our Lord replied "I tell you the truth, today you will be with me in paradise."

Because of this last statement, many Christians believe that this criminal was immediately transported to heaven upon death. However, that is not the case. Many may be somewhat taken aback by such a bold statement, but such a bold statement can be made quite simply because our Lord Himself was not taken to heaven upon His death ... so how could he say "*today* you will be with me in paradise"?

First of all, before His death, our Lord stated that "as Jonah was three days and three nights in the belly of a huge fish, so the Son of Man will be three days and three nights in the heart of the earth," (Matthew 12:40). Here our Lord Himself stated that He was to spend the time between His death and resurrection in "the heart of the earth".

Furthermore, just after His resurrection He told Mary "Do not hold on to me." And the reason He gave her for not doing so was "For I have not yet returned to the Father." Thus He had not yet ascended into heaven.

These two statements, alone, show that our Lord had not returned to heaven during the period of time between His death and resurrection, and the *Apostles' Creed* acknowledges this also, when it says that He "died and was buried, *he descended to the dead*. On the third day he rose again, he ascended into heaven."

What causes the problem?

The problem is caused by a little comma! In Luke 23:43 the translators have placed the comma in the wrong place. There is no punctuation in the Greek and each individual translator can put in whatever punctuation he thinks best. If we move the comma one word, the result would be: "I tell you the truth today, you will be with me in paradise." In other words our Lord was promising the criminal a place in paradise, but he was not going to be there that very day.[8]

I tell you the truth today!

Now the expression "I tell you the truth today" was a common expression, used to emphasise what the person was saying, as we might say to someone, "I'm telling you now, I'm going to apply for a new job." We are not saying "now (at this moment) I am going to apply for a new job". We make the expression "I'm telling you" more emphatic by placing "now" on the end. And it is the same in the Bible. "Today" or "This day" is used in many places at the end of a variety of expressions. For instance they are used 42 times in Deuteronomy alone. Consider the following from Deuteronomy 4:25-26:

> After you have had children and grandchildren and have lived in the land a long time - if you then become corrupt and make any kind of idol, doing evil in the eyes of the LORD your God and provoking him to anger, I call heaven and earth as witnesses against you *this day* that you will quickly perish from the land that you are crossing the Jordan to possess. You will not live there long but will certainly be destroyed.

Here there is no punctuation. However, we can see that "this day" clearly goes with what has gone before: i.e. "I call upon heaven and earth as witnesses against you this day." Moses was most definitely *not* saying

---

[8] For more on this subject see *The Path to Immortality* by Roland Wicks, *The Life and Soul of Mortal Man* by Charles Ozanne, and *Asleep in Christ* by Helaine Burch.

"this day you will quickly perish from the land." Rather he was emphasising that judgment might fall upon them sometime in the future, if they became corrupt and made idols and did evil. It is the same in Luke 23:43. The Lord is not saying to the criminal "Today you will be with me in paradise". Rather, for emphasis, He says, "I tell you the truth today," and what He emphasises is that sometime in the future the criminal will be with the Lord in paradise. Such emphasis would reassure the thief.

More examples

Deuteronomy 5:1 states, "Moses summoned all Israel and said: 'Hear, O Israel, the decrees and the laws I declare in your hearing today. Learn them and be sure to follow them.'" Here, the punctuation is correct. Moses was not saying, "Today learn them and be sure to follow them." They were to follow them all the days of their lives. The expression "Today" is added to a statement to give it emphasis, to make it a solemn statement. This is just what our Lord did in Luke 23:43.

Deuteronomy 6:6 states, "These commandments that I give you today are to be upon your hearts." Again, even though there is no punctuation we can see that "today" goes with "These commandments that I give you", rather than "today" the commandments "are to be upon your hearts." He wanted the commandments to be upon their hearts every day throughout their lives, not just today.

And there are many more such example throughout the Old Testament (e.g. Deuteronomy 7:11 and 8:1).

Conclusion

Neither our Lord nor the criminal entered paradise on the day that they were crucified. Our Lord spent the next three days and nights in the earth, as He said He would. Then came His resurrection, and forty days later He ascended into heaven. The criminal still awaits his resurrection, an event which takes place when Christ returns. Then he shall enter the paradise that Christ promised, His kingdom upon this earth.

9 The Great Commission is our commission
True or false?

Matthew 28:18-20

Then Jesus came to them and said, "All authority in heaven and on earth has been given to me. Therefore go and make disciples of all nations, baptizing them in the name of the Father and of the Son and of the Holy Spirit, and teaching them to obey everything I have commanded you. And surely I am with you always, to the very end of the age."

The words from Matthew 28:18-20 are termed *The Great Commission* and are seen by many as marching orders not only for the Apostles, but also for the church of this dispensation. They, and we, should go out and preach, teach and baptise people from all nations. If that interpretation is correct, some ask, why were the disciples so reluctant to carry out Christ's orders? Especially as Christ repeated those instructions in Acts 1:8 when He said, "You will be my witnesses in Jerusalem, and in all Judea and Samaria, and to the ends of the earth."

Now Scripture makes no bones about the weaknesses of its leading characters: David with Bathsheba; Paul and Barnabas arguing so ferociously that they parted company; Peter denying the Lord three times; and later refusing to eat with Gentiles. However, I have found in Peter a soul-mate. On the spur of the moment, like any of us, he can say or do the wrong thing. However, given time to think, not only does Peter *know* what is right, he *does* it. Even though he had refused to eat with Gentiles in Antioch, and had to be reprimanded by Paul (Galatians 2:11-21), a little while later he totally supported Paul's position with respect to the Gentile Christians at the Jerusalem Council (Acts 15:7-11).

Thus we have to ask ourselves, was Peter really reluctant to carry out the Great Commission? (And not only Peter, but also John, Matthew and the rest of the Twelve. And also James, the Lord's half-brother, and many others!) If we have to attribute wrong behaviour to so many leading people over so many years then perhaps our understanding of the Scriptures is incorrect.

Matthew 28:18-20

It has been suggested that the words "go and make disciples *of* all nations" should be rendered "go and make disciples *out of* all nations". This may well be correct for the Greek says simply, "disciple all nations". However, who, at that point of time, would the Twelve have understood they should go to? I think the answer is clearly ... Jews; and especially Jews of the dispersion. Why do I say that?

For forty days after His resurrection the Lord Jesus appeared to them and taught them and "opened their minds so that they could understand the Scriptures" (Luke 24:45). And having been taught by the Perfect Teacher, and having been given understanding of the Scriptures, the question they asked was "Lord, are you at this time going to *restore* the kingdom to *Israel*?" (Acts 1:6).

So it may well have been the case that at that time the Lord wanted them to disciple only Jews in other Nations: i.e. Jews of the dispersion. Peter, James, John, and Jude all wrote letters to the Jews of the dispersion.

The Lord also went on to tell them "you will be my witnesses in Jerusalem, and in all Judea and Samaria, and to the ends of the earth" (Acts 1:8). So at the start of Acts it seems that what the Lord wanted them to do was to be His witnesses in Jerusalem, and there, in that city, to disciple the dispersion of Israel. And that is precisely what they did do!

Acts

In Jerusalem on the day of Pentecost we read that "there were staying in Jerusalem God-fearing Jews from *every nation* under heaven" (Acts 2:5). The Twelve witnessed to these Jews and about three thousand were saved (Acts 2:41). They continued their witness and the number grew to five thousand (Acts 4:4). By the time we reach Acts 21:20, James can say, "You see, brother, how many thousands of Jews have believed, and all of them are zealous for the law." And the Greek is *murias,* which means myriads; i.e. fifty thousand, tens of thousands, innumerable.

When Peter, James and John met Paul and Barnabas they made an agreement that Paul and Barnabas should go to the Gentiles while they would go to the Jews (Galatians 2:9). Now if we interpret that racially we find this not to be true. Everywhere Paul and Barnabas went, they went first to the synagogue of the Jews. Thus it makes more sense to interpret Galatians 2:9 geographically: i.e. that Paul and Barnabas would go into the Gentile nations while Peter, James and John would stay in Jerusalem and Judea.

But why the Jews?

But why did the Lord want so much effort put into witnessing to the Jews at that time? The Twelve were to stay in Jerusalem and Judea, witnessing to the locals and to the dispersion who visited the Temple; Paul and Barnabas were to witness to the Jews in the synagogues of the dispersion. Remember the question the disciples asked: "Lord, are you at this time going to restore the kingdom to *Israel*?"

God's plan was for Israel to be a special people, a kingdom of priests, and as such to take the message of Himself to the other (Gentile) nations (Exodus 19:5-6). However, they rejected their Messiah for a variety of reasons but on the cross Christ prayed, "Father, forgive them, for they do not know what they are doing?" (Luke 23:34). If that prayer was for the people of Israel, (and it was), then it makes the disciples' question in Acts 1:6 very understandable. Will the kingdom be restored to Israel? Will they now become the kingdom of priests?

Just as Christ's ministry, when He was on earth, was focused almost entirely upon the people of Israel, it is so with the ministry of the Twelve. It is not a case of their being reluctant to go to the Gentiles; it is rather that they should be Christ's witnesses in Jerusalem and Judea first of all, and make disciples from the Jews of the dispersion who came from the different nations. That was their commission, that was the plan, and that is precisely what they did.

However, there was also growing opposition, generally from the Jewish leadership and, particularly, from one Saul of Tarsus. For safety the Christian Jews (except for the Apostles) fled from Jerusalem into Samaria, a place where the Lord Himself had been and they witnessed there. But the opposition had left its mark, and it seems that the response from the Jewish nation was not well. The plan was for this Nation to be converted and to become missionaries to the rest of the world, but the leadership, in particular, were not responding. What was God going to do?

At last Gentiles

And so God chose to send Peter to Cornelius! Why? And God commissioned Paul not only to go to the people of Israel, but also to the Gentiles (Acts 9:15). Why? Israel as a nation had not become a Kingdom of Priests, so why start going to the Gentiles? Why not wait a little longer? Israel might respond.

God, however, knew that the nation of Israel had partially hardened its heart against Christ (Romans 11:25), and so He had planned to do something new. He decided to bring in the Gentiles in order to provoke Israel and so save them (Romans 11:11-14). This was the reason for Gentile salvation at that time, (during the period covered by the Acts of the Apostles), but obviously it is not the reason for Gentile salvation today.[9]

That God would do such a new thing understandably caught Peter unawares and explains his reluctance to go to Cornelius (Acts 10). It also explains why the Jewish Christians in Jerusalem questioned Peter about going to Cornelius, and why they sent Barnabas to Antioch when the Greeks there started to believe in Jesus (Acts 11:1-3,19-22).

---

[9] For more on this subject, please see chapter 26 and 27 of this book.

Did it work?

If we read through the Acts we find in many places that Paul, having preached to the Jews in the synagogues, met with a mixed reaction: some believed but others opposed him. He then turned to Gentiles and this often provoked envy in the Jewish community. Sadly, such envy resulted in abuse and sometimes violence, rather than salvation (e.g. Acts 13:45).

By the time we get to the end of the Acts we find that the partial hardening had become so complete that Israel were now deaf to any preaching about Jesus and blind to the Scriptures which showed Him to be the Christ, the Son of God (Acts 28:25-28). As a result Israel lost its place as the premier nation in God's plan. They could not, at that time, become a kingdom of priests to the other nations of the world and so we read that "God's salvation has been sent to the Gentiles, and they will listen" (Acts 28:28). And listen they did.

Less than a year later Paul wrote to the Colossians and stated:

> My fellow prisoner Aristarchus sends you his greetings, as does Mark, the cousin of Barnabas. (You have received instructions about him; if he comes to you, welcome him.) Jesus, who is called Justus, also sends greetings. These are **the only Jews** among my fellow workers for the kingdom of God, and they have proved a comfort to me.

Within a generation the Christian world was almost entirely Gentile, and when we reach the next century we have the writings of the Early Church Fathers, all of whom are Gentiles; there is not one Jew amongst them.

Part 2

Comments and Queries about the Acts of the Apostles

10 Paul should have replaced Judas
True or false?

Acts 1:15-26

In those days Peter stood up among the believers (a group numbering about a hundred and twenty) and said, "Brothers, the Scripture had to be fulfilled which the Holy Spirit spoke long ago through the mouth of David concerning Judas, who served as guide for those who arrested Jesus - he was one of our number and shared in this ministry." (With the reward he got for his wickedness, Judas bought a field; there he fell headlong, his body burst open and all his intestines spilled out. Everyone in Jerusalem heard about this, so they called that field in their language Akeldama, that is, Field of Blood.)

"For," said Peter, "it is written in the book of Psalms, "'May his place be deserted; let there be no one to dwell in it,' and, 'May another take his place of leadership.' Therefore it is necessary to choose one of the men who have been with us the whole time the Lord Jesus went in and out among us, beginning from John's baptism to the time when Jesus was taken up from us. For one of these must become a witness with us of his resurrection."

So they proposed two men: Joseph called Barsabbas (also known as Justus) and Matthias. Then they prayed, "Lord, you know everyone's heart. Show us which of these two you have chosen to take over this apostolic ministry, which Judas left to go where he belongs." Then they cast lots, and the lot fell to Matthias; so he was added to the eleven apostles.

Our Lord Jesus chose Twelve Disciples and these are to have a special role when He returns and sets up His kingdom upon the earth. He told them, "I tell you the truth, at the renewal of all things, when the Son of Man sits on his glorious throne, you who have followed me will also sit on twelve thrones, judging the twelve tribes of Israel" (Matthew 19:28).

However, Judas betrayed the Lord and committed suicide. It was therefore necessary to make the number back up to twelve; another was to "take his place of leadership", or "office" as the *ASV* has (Acts 1:20), but who could it be?

We know from the start of Acts that the disciples came up with two people: Matthias and Joseph called Barsabbas, but having been told Matthias was the one selected, we read nothing more of him in the rest of the New Testament! And neither do we hear any more of this Joseph! That being the case, and Paul being the dominant disciple in the rest of the New Testament, some have concluded that Peter and company acted hastily and made a wrong decision; they should have been patient and waited for Paul to come on the scene.

Making decisions

I do not see Peter and the Twelve as perfect people. The Scriptures are not reluctant to let us know of the weaknesses of some of the leading people of God. However, when it comes to 'committee' meetings and making 'policy' decisions (e.g. the Jerusalem Council of Acts 15), they are much more likely to have corporately been correct than people living 2,000 years after the event. Not only that, Christ had made them a special promise.

> "I tell you the truth, whatever you bind on earth will be bound in heaven, and whatever you loose on earth will be loosed in heaven. Again, I tell you that if two of you on earth agree about anything you ask for, it will be done for you by my Father in heaven. For where two or three come together in my name, there am I with them." (Matthew 18:18-21)

I have dealt with this verse extensively in *40 Problem Passages*, (available from the Open Bible Trust). The expressions "binding" and "loosing" were terms used for making synagogue rules and appointments. What Christ promised the apostles was that when they came together to make decisions, He would be with them and so their decisions, what they bound and what they loosed, would be sanctioned by heaven. Thus in selecting Matthias they made the right choice.

More reasons

But there are other reasons why Paul could not have been the replacement for Judas. The Twelve had to be *eyewitnesses* of Christ's life to the people of Israel. Thus, as Peter states, such an eyewitness had to be a person who had been with them "the whole time the Lord Jesus went in and out among us, **beginning from** John's baptism **to the time when** Jesus was taken up from us" (Acts 1:21-22). Whether this meant that the Twelve were present at Christ's baptism and heard the voice from heaven saying "This is my Son, whom I love; with him I am well pleased" is a possibility, and if so then both Matthias and Joseph must have been there also … but Paul was not.

They also had to have been there at the ascension and, again, clearly Matthias and Joseph had been, but Paul had not.

And they also had to have been eyewitnesses of the physical resurrection of Christ (Acts 1:22). Again, Matthias and Joseph had been, but Paul had not.

Casting Lots[10]

However, having reduced the short-list to two people, the disciples were then unable to decide which of the two was the right one. To solve their problem they sought the Lord's answer by casting lots. This was not some random, haphazard way of abrogating their human responsibility. Rather it was the right way for Jews, at that time, to seek God's will on such a matter for, as Proverbs 16:33 states, "The lot is cast into the lap, but its every decision is from the Lord."

---

[10] For more on casting lots see *The Miracles of the Apostles* by Michael Penny published by the Open Bible Trust.

Thus there is extensive evidence to show that Peter and company were correct to replace Judas with Matthias and not to wait for Paul. Furthermore, the Twelve were the Apostles to Israel. Paul, on the other hand, is the only person called *The Apostle to the Gentiles* (Romans 11:13; Galatians 2:8).

11 Pentecost is the *birthday* of the Church
True or false?

I suppose the predominant view in Christendom is that "The church began at Pentecost", but ... did it? After all, Pentecost was a Jewish feast, one of the big ones, so why would the Lord choose a Jewish Feast day to begin something new: a predominantly Gentile church?

In fact Pentecost was one of several feasts listed in Leviticus 23, which formed the basis of Israel's religious calendar. As well as the weekly Sabbath there were the seven annual feasts or festivals: Passover and Unleavened Bread; First fruits; Pentecost, also called the Feast of Weeks; Trumpets, Atonement, and Tabernacles. Each feast, as well as remembering a past event, also looked forward to a future one.

Passover and Unleavened Bread

> This is the feast of Pentecost – the type of God's people, gathered by the Holy Ghost, and presented before Him, in connection with all the preciousness of Christ. In the Passover we have the death of Christ, in the sheaf of first-fruits we have the resurrection of Christ, and in the feast of Pentecost we have the descent of the Holy Ghost to form the Church. All this is divinely perfect. The death and resurrection of Christ had to be accomplished ere the Church could be formed.
>
> (C.H. Mackintosh, p 402 *Notes on the Pentateuch*)

Not only did these two look back to the Exodus and the Passover lamb when Israel put all leaven (yeast) outside the home, they also looked forward to the future and were fulfilled in our Lord Jesus Christ's death; His sacrifice for sin. As Paul put it in 1 Corinthians 5:7-8, "For Christ, our Passover lamb, has been sacrificed. Therefore let us keep the

Festival, not with the old yeast, the yeast of malice and wickedness, but with bread without yeast, the bread of sincerity and truth."

Firstfruits

The sheaf of the firstfruits of the harvest was to be waved before the Lord on the day after the Sabbath; the first day of the week. This was the day when our Lord Jesus was raised from the dead. He was *the* firstfruits, as 1 Corinthians 15:20-23 makes clear: "But Christ has indeed been raised from the dead, the firstfruits of those who have fallen asleep. For since death came through a man, the resurrection of the dead comes also through a man. For as in Adam all die, so in Christ all will be made alive. But each in his own turn: Christ, the firstfruits; then, when he comes, those who belong to him."

However, there were also others who believed in Him on that day, and on the days following. During the weeks before His ascension more and more believed and formed the first fruits of the harvest that was to come.

Pentecost

This came fifty days after Pentecost and Unleavened Bread, when an offering of new grain was made to the Lord. On that Day of Pentecost in Acts 2, the 120 Jews who believed in Christ were that new grain. And the Holy Spirit descended upon them, and the harvest from Israel began with 3,000 that day, and it was not long until that number of men who believed grew to 5,000 (Acts 2:42; 4:4).

Trumpets and Atonement

The Feast of Trumpets, just ten days before Atonement, was celebrated by trumpet blasts and announced to the nation of Israel the coming of the Day of Atonement, when the high priest made atonement for the sins of the Nation of Israel. These two events await future fulfilments with Israel. We read of the trumpet blasts in Revelation 8-11, and as Christ returns the last trumpet is sounded and the dead are raised (1 Corinthians 15:52; 1 Thessalonians 4:16). Then Israel enter their great Day of

Atonement, when they look on Him whom they pierced and rejected (Revelation 1:7). They repent, are given a new heart, and the nation is born again in a day (Ezekiel 36:24-34). This is followed by ...

Tabernacles

This feast not only remembered the time when Israel lived in tents (tabernacles) in the wilderness. It also looked forward to the 1,000 year Millennial Kingdom of Christ upon this earth; an event which will follow His return (Revelation 20:4).

All the feasts

As every one of the feasts is intimately linked with the people of Israel (both in their history and also in their prophecy) it seems incongruent that one of them – the Day of Pentecost – should be singled out for the beginning of the church which became almost exclusively Gentile.

Not only that, in the period of time following the completion of the Old Testament, Pentecost came to

> The foundation of the seven feasts was Grace; the top-stone, Glory; for the Passover proclaimed redemption through the blood, and the last feast – Tabernacles, pictured the Millennium. Between these two feasts came the sheaf of the First-Fruits, i.e. the Resurrection of Christ; Pentecost, i.e. the Descent of the Holy Spirit upon the Firstfruits themselves; and the Great Day of Atonement when they shall look upon Him whom they have pierced, and repentant, receive the new heart predicted in Ezekiel.
>
> George Williams, p 75 *The Student's Commentary*

be regarded as the anniversary of the giving of the Law at Sinai (Babylonian Talmud, *Pesahim* 68B; Midrash, *Tanhuma* 26c). Thus those Jews who met in Jerusalem on the Day of Pentecost came, not only to celebrate the new harvest, but also to remember the giving of the Law of Moses to the people of Israel.

Also, if we read the Scriptures, we see that the inspired writers almost go out of their way to make it clear that the events described pertain solely to the people of Israel. For example, it tells us "staying in Jerusalem were God-fearing Jews from every nation under heaven" (Acts 2:5). It goes on to repeat that the people there were "Jews and converts to Judaism" (2: 11).

Peter, when speaking to them, addresses them as "Fellow Jews" (2:14), "Men of Israel" (2:22), "Brothers" (2:29), and concludes by saying "Let all Israel be assured ...." (2:36). The simple fact is that Scripture does not record the presence of even a single Gentile present to witness the events which took place on that Day of Pentecost described in Acts 2.

And in his speech Peter quotes from the prophecy of Joel (2:28-32), and the Psalms (16:8-11; 110:1). The Gentiles of that time would not have known of these Scriptures and certainly would not have understood them.

Conclusion

If the almost exclusively Gentile church of this age did not begin at Pentecost, at the start of Acts, when did it begin? The answer is quite simple[11]: at the end of Acts, after the sixth and final pronouncement of Isaiah's judgmental prophecy upon Israel. Because that nation had hardened its heart against Jesus, rejecting Him as both Christ (Messiah) and Son of God (see Acts 28:25-27), they became blind and deaf and useless. Thus God sent His salvation to the Gentiles, who were not only to listen, but who were, in time, to take the gospel message of salvation by grace through faith in Christ Jesus to the ends of the earth.

---

[11] For a fuller treatment of this subject read *The Church! When did it begin? And why is it important?* By Olive and Lloyd Allen, available from The Open Bible Trust.

12 Breaking bread is the Lord's Supper True or false?

Considering the importance given by many churches to the Lord's Supper, it is surprising just how infrequently it is mentioned in the New Testament. We read about it in Matthew, Mark and Luke, but interestingly John does not record it in his Gospel.

There is no reference to it in the Acts of the Apostles and it is mentioned in only one of the epistles, namely 1 Corinthians. However, whatever it was the Corinthians were celebrating in their meetings they were told by Paul, "When you come together, it is *not* the Lord's Supper you eat" (1 Corinthians 11:20).

When we take a closer look at that letter, we see that this reference to the Lord's Supper comes within a section written specifically to Jewish Christians; 1 Corinthians 10:1 – 11:33. How do we know that this is a section for Jewish Christians?

1 Corinthians 10:1-2 states, "I do not want you to be ignorant of the fact, brothers, *that our forefathers* were all under the cloud and that they all passed through the sea. They were all baptised into Moses in the cloud and in the sea." This is clearly referring to the Jewish Christians, but when we get to the start of Chapter 12 we read, "Now about spiritual gifts, brothers, I do not want you to be ignorant. You know that when you were *pagans*, somehow or other you were influenced and led astray to mute idols," (1 Corinthians 12:1).

Thus the section between 1 Corinthians 10:1 and 1 Corinthians 12:1 deals with issues and problems relating to Jewish Christians. This is supported by references to judgments[12] falling on some of them. Because of gluttony and drunkenness at this meal, Paul wrote, "That is why many among you are weak and sick, and a number of you have fallen asleep,"

---

[12] For more on the miracle of judgment and its significance see chapter 14 of *The Miracles of the Apostles* by Michael Penny and available from the Open Bible Trust.

(1 Corinthians 11:30). We do not read in the New Testament of such judgments falling upon Gentiles, but only upon Jews: for example, Ananias and Sapphira were Jewish Christians and were struck dead; Herod Agrippa was a Jew and was struck dead; Elymas was a Jew and was struck blind (see Acts 5:1-11; 12:19-23; 13:6-11).

Again, we should note carefully what we read in 1 Corinthians 11. Whatever the Christian Jews in Corinth were doing, Paul told them that "it is *not* the Lord's Supper you eat" (1 Corinthians 11:20).

Breaking Bread in Acts

Because these are the only references to the Lord's Supper in the New Testament some have stated that where we have references to people 'breaking bread' this expression refers to the Lord's Supper. Notable amongst these was J N Darby, and the Brethren's Lord's Supper was called *The Breaking of Bread*. We find the following four references to expressions such as this in Acts.

> They devoted themselves to the apostles' teaching and to the fellowship, to the *breaking of bread* and to prayer. (Acts 2:42)

> Every day they continued to meet together in the temple courts. They *broke bread* in their homes and ate together with glad and sincere hearts. (Acts 2:46)

> On the first day of the week we came together *to break bread*. Paul spoke to the people and, because he intended to leave the next day, kept on talking until midnight. There were many lamps in the upstairs room where we were meeting. Seated in a window was a young man named Eutychus, who was sinking into a deep sleep as Paul talked on and on. When he was sound asleep, he fell to the ground from the third story and was picked up dead.

Paul went down, threw himself on the young man and put his arms around him. "Don't be alarmed," he said. "He's alive!" Then he went upstairs again and *broke bread* and ate. After talking until daylight, he left. (Acts 20:7-11)

After he said this, he took some *bread* and gave thanks to God in front of them all. Then he *broke* it and began to eat. (Acts 27:35)

So do these references refer to the Lord's Supper or not? We will return to that question in a moment.

Breaking Bread before the Last Supper

At the feeding of the 5,000 we read:

And he directed the people to sit down on the grass. Taking the five *loaves* and the two fish and looking up to heaven, he gave thanks and *broke the loaves* ... They all ate and were satisfied. (Matthew 14:19-20; see also Mark 6:41-42 and Luke 9:16-17.)

And we find exactly the same expression in the feeding of the 4,000: our Lord *broke* the *loaves* ... and they all ate (Matthew 15:36-37; see also Mark 8:6-8). Later, when referring to this miracle, our Lord asked, "When I *broke* the five *loaves* for the five thousand, how many basketfuls of pieces did you pick up?" (Mark 8:19)

These 'loaves' of bread were not 'loaves' in our sense of the word. They were thin cakes, almost like pancakes, which were not cut, but were broken or torn before being eaten. Hence the idiom 'to break bread' meant 'to have a meal', and we see this in the Old Testament.

Neither shall men *break bread* for them in mourning; neither shall men give them the cup of consolation to drink for their father or their mother. (Isaiah 16:7; *KJV*, margin)

The tongue of the sucking child cleaveth to the roof of his mouth for thirst: the young children ask [for] *bread,* and no man *breaketh* it unto them. (Lamentations 4:4; *KJV*).

Sometimes, instead of the word 'break' we have the word 'tear', but the sense is the same. So by New Testament times 'to break bread' was a well-used idiom for a meal. We see this in the feeding of the 5,000, and the 4,000, and clearly none of these can refer to the Lord's Supper. The same expression is also used when we read of our Lord having a meal with the two He met on the Emmaus road we read:

When he was at the table with them, he took *bread*, gave thanks, *broke* it and began to give it to them ... Then the two told what had happened on the way, and how Jesus was recognised by them when he *broke the bread.* (Luke 24:30,35)

Breaking Bread at the Last Supper

The occasion of the Last Supper was the Passover[13]. However, this was a meal, the Passover Meal, and so we should not be surprised to read that at this meal "Jesus took bread, gave thanks and *broke* it," (Mark 14:22; see also Matthew 26:26 and Luke 22:19)

Breaking Bread in Acts

Thus we must return to the question we posed earlier: do the references to 'breaking bread' in the Acts of the Apostles refer to the Lord's Supper or do they simply refer to people having a meal together?

Clearly the reference in Acts 27:35 cannot refer to the Lord's Supper. Paul was on a pagan ship, bound for Rome, chained to a Roman soldier and surrounded by unbelieving Gentiles. They were in the middle of a storm and the fact that this is a meal is borne out by what we read: "Then

---

[13] For a detailed account of what went on at a Passover Meal and how the Lord's Supper relates to it see chapter 5 in *Think on these things* by Ernest Streets, available from the Open Bible Trust.

he *broke* it and began to *eat*. They were all encouraged and *ate* some food themselves," (Acts 27:35-36).

The account in Acts 20:7-11, where Paul raised Eutychus, is again a meal. It refers to their coming together 'on the first day of the week'. In Jewish time 'the first day of the week' started at sunset on Saturday, so this would have been the Saturday evening meal. After they had eaten Paul talked until midnight and Eutychus fell from the third floor. Paul raised him and then went back upstairs and had some more to eat: he "*broke bread* and ***ate***". Having spoken for several hours, and having then had the trauma involving Eutychus, one can well imagine that Paul was in need of further sustenance.

And similarly we read in Acts 2:46 that:

> ... they *broke bread* in their homes and ***ate*** together.

Thus the general conclusion must therefore be that in the Bible, both in the Old Testament and the New, expressions such as 'breaking bread' refer to the eating of a meal. It is not surprising that 'breaking of bread' occurred at the Last Supper. This was, after all, the occasion of the Passover Meal.

13 Gentiles were saved at Pentecost True or false?

I have been reading about a church where one of the leaders, away on a ministry trip, went into the home of a person who was not fully accepted in the community. During the visit the minister shared the gospel and the man, and his family, responded to the message and all became believers in the Lord Jesus Christ. However, when the leader returned home, he was questioned and then criticised by his church for having visited such a person.

Can you believe this? Well I can, because I read about it. No! Not in a newspaper or a magazine, but in the Bible. The leader was Peter. The person was Cornelius. And the church was in Jerusalem – see Acts 11:1-18. What was going on here?

A common error

One of the common errors leading to a misunderstanding of the Bible is to read truth revealed at one time into earlier books of the Bible. For example, if Abraham lived to be 175 years, and there are 52 weeks in a year, how many Sabbaths did Abraham keep? This is not an exercise in arithmetic because the answer is zero. Abraham lived 400 years before the Law was given to Moses. Thus we are wrong to read Sabbath Law back into Genesis or into the earlier parts of Exodus.

It is true that God wanted the message of salvation to go to the Gentiles, but when did that come about?

God's revealed plan up to that time

During the Old Testament, the Gospels and the first part of the period of time covered by the Acts of the Apostles, there were three strands of teaching which concerned the Gentiles.

(1) First there was the Abrahamic Covenant of Genesis 12:1-3, in which God said "I will bless those who bless you." That is, Gentiles who helped Jews were to be blessed by God.

(2) Second, as time went by, it became possible for Gentiles to join themselves to the people of Israel. To do this they had to be circumcised, observe the Sabbath, and do their best to keep the rest of the Mosaic Law, just like any Jew: see Isaiah 56:3-7. Such Gentile converts to Judaism were known as 'Proselytes'.

(3) And there was the ultimate plan: Israel were to become a Kingdom of Priests to the Gentile Nations, teaching them about the Lord: see Exodus 19:4-6.

The Abrahamic Covenant

We continue to see this in operation when our Lord was on earth. When He came to Capernaum there was a Gentile Centurion whose servant was ill and needed healing. The leaders of the Jews came to Christ and said to Him, "This man deserves to have you do this, because he loves our nation and has built our synagogue" (Luke 7:4-5). And our Lord healed his servant.

The same was true with Cornelius, of whom we read, "He and all his family were devout and God-fearing; he gave generously to those in need and prayed to God regularly" (Acts 10:2). As he was stationed in Caesarea in Judea the poor to whom he gave were obviously Jewish poor.

Proselytes and God-fearers

When our Lord was on earth, and during the Acts period, a number of thinking Gentiles became disillusioned with the emptiness and hypocrisy of pagan worship. Drunkenness was the mode of worship in the temple of Bacchus; the temple of Zeus in Corinth had 1,000 priestesses, (prostitutes in reality), and intercourse was considered an act of worship; orgies figured in some temples.

However, throughout that Greco-Roman world there was a hard-working, moralistic group of people. Their worship consisted of singing songs, praying, reading from some scrolls and listening to someone talk about the reading. Slowly a number of Gentiles started to attend the synagogues and in some places the numbers became so great, that when new synagogues were built they included special sections for these Gentiles: they were known as God-fearers.

If these God-fearers took the step of being circumcised, and kept the Sabbath, they became known as Proselytes and were fully embraced into both Jewish religion and society: they could enter the main body of the synagogue and the inner courts of the temple in Jerusalem. However, God-fearers, while welcome in the synagogue, were not welcomed into Jewish homes and it was not acceptable for Jews to visit their homes. The teaching of the Pharisees (but not that of the Law of Moses) was that all Gentiles were unclean[14]. Cornelius was a God-fearer (Acts 10:2), and we read of many more in the synagogues Paul visited.

The Kingdom of Priests

However, the greater plan for the Gentiles would be fulfilled only when Israel became a kingdom of priests and this was on the mind of the disciples when, at the start of Acts, they asked, "Lord, are you at this time going to restore the kingdom to Israel?" (Acts 1:6). His reply was evasive, but He did direct them ... to Jerusalem first, then Judea, then Samaria and then, ultimately, the ends of the earth (Acts 1:8).

They embarked on this work, initially gaining thousands of converts (Acts 2:41; 4:4), but opposition arose, headed by the Jewish leadership, and the Christians, apart from the Apostles, fled Jerusalem (Acts 8:1).

---

[14] In Acts 10:28 when Peter visited Cornelius he said, "You are well aware that it is against our law for a Jew to associate with a Gentile." However, the word translated 'law' here is not *nomos*, the word for the Law of Moses. Rather it is the word *themis*; i.e. custom, and was used of the Pharisaic additions to the Law of Moses.

Thus the task of converting Israel, and of their becoming a kingdom of priests, was faltering so ... was it time to go to the Gentiles? Not yet!

A new thing

It was no secret what God would do if the nation of Israel did not fully obey the Law; Deuteronomy 28:15-68 spells out the judgments. Isaiah 6:8-13 also made it clear that, if Israel hardened its hearts and became blind and deaf, it would be cut down like a tree, and taken into exile – which is just what happened at the hands of the Babylonians.

However, during Acts there was now a different problem in Israel: some believed and some opposed. The nation was stumbling (but not beyond recovery) and "Israel has experienced a hardening in part," is how Paul described their condition in Romans 11:11,25. What was God going to do about this? Romans 11:11-27 provides the answer.

Gentiles saved

God sent certain people (such as Peter) to the Gentiles and His reason for doing so was to arouse Israel, to provoke them, and so to save them.

> Again I ask: did they stumble so as to fall beyond recovery? Not at all! Rather, because of their transgression, salvation has come to the Gentiles to make Israel envious. But if their transgression means riches for the world, and their loss means riches for the Gentiles, how much greater riches will their full inclusion bring!
> I am talking to you Gentiles. Inasmuch as I am the apostle to the Gentiles, I take pride in my ministry in the hope that I may somehow arouse my own people to envy and save some of them. (Romans 11:11-14)

The analogy given in Romans 11 is that of a wild olive branch (the Gentiles) being grafted into the cultivated olive tree (Israel). In olive farming this would frequently result in the cultivated olive tree producing more and better fruit. This was God's desire for Israel, but His doing this was something new and had been kept a secret (a better word than 'mystery' in Romans 11:25). If all this is the case, we can well understand Peter's reluctance to go to Cornelius in the first place and the Jerusalem church for questioning him about it.

We must, however, make it clear that this was the reason for Gentile salvation *at that time*: during the period covered by the Acts of the Apostles. The provoking of Israel to salvation (Romans 11:11-14) is **not** the reason why Gentiles are saved today.

Did it work?

As we read through the Acts of the Apostles we see the Jews being aroused in a number of places. Some did believe while others were provoked, but not into believing that Jesus was the Messiah (Christ), the Son of God: rather they became jealous, abusive and violent (Acts 13:45). And throughout the rest of the Acts of the Apostles this situation continued, as we see, for example, in the treatment of Paul in Lystra, where he was stoned (Acts 14:19). However, this situation could not go on and on for ever, and it seems that slowly the opposition grew.

When we get to the end of Acts we read the final pronouncement of Isaiah's judgmental prophecy.

> They disagreed among themselves and began to leave after Paul had made this final statement: "The Holy Spirit spoke the truth to your ancestors when he said through Isaiah the prophet:
> 'Go to this people and say, You will be ever hearing but never understanding; you will be ever seeing but never perceiving.'
> For this people's heart has become calloused; they hardly hear with their ears, and they have closed their eyes. Otherwise they might see with their eyes, hear with their ears, understand with their hearts and turn, and I would heal them." (Acts 28:25-27)

Israel had now hardened its heart. It was deaf to the teachings of the Apostles and blind to the Scriptures which clearly showed that Jesus was the Christ, the Son of God. Given that situation it is not surprising that, just as years earlier that nation had been taken into exile by the Babylonians, Israel were soon exiled throughout the Roman Empire, when the Romans destroyed the city and the temple in AD 70.

What was God going to do now?

Following the quotation from Isaiah 6 in Acts 28:25-27, we read in verse 28 that, "God's salvation has been sent to the Gentiles and they will listen." And listen they did. When Christian history opens at the start of the second century we find that the early church fathers were all Gentiles. There was not one Jew amongst them.

14 Philippi was the first place in Europe where the Gospel was preached
True or false?

I have heard it from pulpits, and I have read it in books. Paul's arrival in Philippi marked the occasion when the gospel first reached Europe; but was that the case?

> The establishment of the church at Philippi, marking as it does, the entrance of the gospel of the Lord Jesus Christ into Europe, is described in Acts 16:12-40 with great fullness of detail.
>
> (p 15, *Philippians, An Introduction and Commentary* by Ralph P Martin, Tyndale New Testament Commentaries published by IVP.)

It is true that this was the first time that Paul, himself, preached the gospel in Europe, but was it "the entrance of the gospel of the Lord Jesus Christ into Europe", as stated by Ralph Martin? Hadn't anyone else, somewhere in Europe, done so before him?

If we continue reading about Paul's second missionary journey, we find him soon leaving Philippi and going on to Thessalonica, where he remained for less than a month. Then, after a short while in Berea, he went on to Athens and soon arrived in Corinth.

> The Church at Philippi held a special place in Paul's heart. Not only was it the first to be established in Europe, but its members proved themselves to be especially faithful, and helped Paul by sending him money at various times.
>
> (Peter Murcott, p 14 *British Church Newspaper*, No.174, December 4 2009)

There he met a Jew named Aquila, a native of Pontus, who had recently come from Italy with his wife Priscilla, because Claudius had ordered all the Jews to leave Rome. (Acts 18:2)

We find that couple were not only Jews, but Christian Jews (Acts 18:24-26), and that they had recently come from Rome. Thus there were Christians in Rome before Paul reached Philippi. Had they not preached the gospel there? It seems that they had.

Claudius expelled the Jews

The Roman historian Suetonius states that Emperor Claudius expelled all the Jews from Rome in 49 AD "because they were constantly rioting at the instigation of Chrestus."

When Christianity was brought to Rome, there were approximately thirteen synagogues in the city; some were open to the teachings of the Christians regarding Jesus Christ (called "Chrestus" by Suetonius), while others fought against those teachings. This tension led to a clash between the synagogues that was so serious that Claudius responded by forcing all 40-50,000 Jews to leave the city.

The Jews expelled by Claudius included not only practitioners of Judaism, but also Jewish Christians. St. Luke tells us that Ss. Aquila and Priscilla went to Corinth (where they met St. Paul) because they were among the Jews expelled by Claudius (Acts 18:2).

The Jews were allowed to return to Rome five years later, at the beginning of Emperor Nero's reign in 54 AD.

(*Be Transformed: An Interactive Study of the Epistle to the Romans* by Jason J. Barker)

In those early days of Christianity the Romans did not clearly distinguish between Christianity and Judaism, considering the former as one of the many branches of the latter. Claudius, who was probably one of the best Caesars Rome had ever had, was a tolerant ruler but did not like any religion proselytising from others, nor fights within a religion. This, apparently, was what the Jews in Rome were doing: the Christian and non-Christian Jews clashed. After being warned they were all expelled. To Claudius it made no difference that some were Christian and some were not; they were all Jews. He expelled the lot. To us, however, it makes a big difference.

But, if there were Christian Jews in Rome preaching the gospel before Paul set sail for Philippi, how did they get there?

God-fearing Jews from every nation

Acts chapter 2 records what happened on the Day of Pentecost following our Lord's ascension. We read that in Jerusalem there were "God-fearing Jews from every nation under heaven" (v 5). In addition, we are told that there were Jews and Proselytes from Rome (verse 10). Proselytes were Gentiles who had converted to Judaism and who had been circumcised and were, to all effects, treated as Jews. (See Isaiah 56:4-7, where the 'covenant' refers to the covenant of circumcision.)

Some fifteen nations are listed, from which we read that about 3,000 became Christians; and in a little while that number had grown to 5,000 men (Acts 2:41; 4:4). Now if those 5,000 were divided equally amongst those fifteen nations it would mean over 300 Jews returning to each place as Christians. However, that is not likely to have been the situation.

There was a very large Jewish community in Egypt and we know that Alexandria in Egypt became one of the great centres of early Christianity, yet we do not read in the New Testament of anyone visiting them; but there were Jews from Egypt present on the Day of Pentecost (Acts 2:10). Neither Peter nor Paul, nor any other apostle, is recorded as ever having visited Egypt, so how was Christianity established there? It seems highly likely that some of the Jews from Egypt became Christians in Jerusalem and took the message back there themselves.

And this is the most likely scenario for Rome also. Soon after the Pentecost of Acts 2 some Jews from Rome, who had become Christians, would have returned home and preached the gospel there, many years before Paul ever set foot on European soil.

Tens of thousands of believers

We should not think that the Day of Pentecost in Acts 2 was an isolated occasion. There were several Jewish feast days each year and many of the Jews of the Dispersion travelled up to Jerusalem. Thus James and the Apostles, who mainly stayed in Jerusalem, had an ever-changing missionary field, and one they worked with much success. In Acts 21:20 we read "see, brother, how many thousands of Jews have believed." But the Greek translated 'thousands' is *murias* which means ten-thousands, and is translated as such by the *KJV*. Thus the 5,000 we read about in Acts 4:4 had grown to tens of thousands by Acts 21.

Similarly, Paul did not establish the church in Colossae, which was in Asia. In fact Paul was prevented by the Holy Spirit from going into Asia (Acts 16:6). There was no need for him to do so, for a church had already been established there by Epaphras (Colossians 1:7); but who was Epahras? On the Day of Pentecost there were Jews from Asia there (Acts 2:9). Was Epahras one of them? If not on that occasion, then he may well have been present on another Jewish feast day later on.

An agreement

In Galatians 2 we read of an agreement: James, Peter and John agreed that they would go to the Jews, while Paul and Barnabas would go to the Gentiles (v 9). However, we should never give the impression that James, Peter and John had less to do or were less successful. They had an ever-changing audience, some of whom were converted to Christ and took the gospel back to their home cities. This was so successful that Paul could write:

> All over the world this gospel is bearing fruit and growing … This is the gospel that you heard and has been proclaimed to every creature under heaven. (Colossians 1:6,23)

And those who took this "all over the world" were not just the Apostles, but relatively unknown Christian Jews. This is most likely how some of the churches were established in such places as Egypt, Asia and Spain, as well as in Rome itself. The gospel was certainly preached there some years before Paul arrived in Philippi. However, whether or not Rome was the first place in Europe to hear the gospel is a different issue.

Post Script: The Church in Egypt

On a holiday in Egypt, one of our guides was a Coptic Christian. He told us that Christianity was brought to Egypt by St. Mark in about AD 64, though I have not been able to verify this.

However, another tradition simply has the Church at Alexandria being established by Mark in the middle of the 1st century (approximately AD 42). Eusebius of Caesarea, the author of Ecclesiastical History in the fourth century, records that Mark went to Egypt in the first or third year of the reign of Emperor Claudius, i.e. 41 or 43 A.D. (See *Two Thousand years of Coptic Christianity*, by Otto F.A. Meinardus p28.)

This would be some years before Mark joined Paul and Barnabas on their first missionary journey to Cyprus, a journey Mark failed to complete (Acts 13:4-13; about AD 47-48).

If Mark did make such a visit to Egypt, it was more likely to visit the Christians already there, rather than to establish the church by being the first person ever to preach the gospel there. As we have seen, on the Day of Pentecost Jews from Egypt (Acts 2:9) were present and it is reasonable to assume that some of them were amongst the 3,000 saved that day, and that they took the gospel back to Egypt and were the first to preach it there.

15 James and Paul were wrong True or false?

There is a view amongst a number of Christians that James was wrong to ask Paul to take a vow, shave his head, go through purification rites, and offer sacrifices; and that Paul was wrong to agree. E.M. Blaiklock in the *Tyndale New Testament Commentary*, describes Paul's action as a 'compromise'. But was it a compromise? And Campbell Morgan, in his book *The Acts of the Apostles*, states that this was "the greatest mistake" of Paul's ministry! But was it? Did James or Paul say or do anything wrong?

This view is based upon another, namely that the Mosaic Law was abolished at the Cross and so there was no reason for James or Paul or any Christian, Jewish or Gentile, to participate in its rules and regulations, its rites and rituals. But is that correct?

They were not perfect

> These elders ... knew that he [Paul] had personally abandoned the observance of rites and ceremonies ... At Antioch he had rebuked Peter for dissimulation, and now they asked him to practice dissimulation ... I hold that Paul made the great*est mistake of his ministry on this occasion.*
>
> (Pages 378-9; *The Acts of the Apostles*, D Campbell Morgan)

The Apostles and leaders were not perfect. They made their mistakes. Peter was wrong when he went to Antioch and stopped eating with Gentiles (Galatians 2:11-13). Paul and Barnabas argued so much that they went their separate ways (Acts 15:36-40). James had not believed Jesus to be the Christ before His resurrection (John 7:5; 1 Corinthians 15:7).

On the spur of the moment, under pressure, they did at times fail. However, in the cold light of morning, when they considered what was the right thing to do or say, they did it. At the Jerusalem Council, a short while after his failure in Antioch, we see Peter totally supporting Paul's stance over the Gentiles (Acts 15:7-11).

James not alone

Now in Acts 21, when Paul returned to Jerusalem after his third missionary journey, Paul reported to 'James, and *all the elders*" (v 18). It was this whole group, not just James, which said to Paul that he should take a vow. Who were in this group of 'elders'? One would suspect people like Peter and John, Matthew and Andrew, and various members of the Twelve. Possibly people like Barnabas. If we have to suggest that a body of people like that were all wrong, in order to justify our interpretation and understanding of Scripture, then I respectfully suggest that 'we' are the ones who are more likely to be wrong.

The background

What caused this situation was that the Christian Jews in Jerusalem had
...

> "... been informed that you [Paul] teach all the Jews who live among the Gentiles to turn away from Moses, telling them not to circumcise their children or live according to our customs." (Acts 21:21)

Was this information correct? Clearly James and the elders did not think it was. Paul had been telling the Gentiles that they need not be circumcised, nor follow the Mosaic Law, nor follow Jewish customs. He was doing this with the blessing of the Jerusalem Council (Acts 15:19-21,23-29).

It is possible that what Paul had been teaching the Gentiles had, somehow or other, been misreported, and it was incorrectly stated that he had been teaching such things to the Jews.

Paul's manner of life

But what of Paul's personal life? Had he been keeping the Mosaic Law? Some theologians maintain that he had not been doing so; that he appreciated that he was free from the Law, and so did not observe it. They go on to state that Paul 'compromised' his true position when he agreed to take the vow. Scripture, however, shows precisely the opposite to be the case. We have only to read through the Acts of the Apostles to see how Paul kept the Law of Moses. Consider, for example, the following:

Sabbath Law

> On the Sabbath day they entered the synagogue ... the next Sabbath ... the next Sabbath. (Acts 13:14,42,44)

> On the Sabbath we went outside the city gate to the river, where we expected to find a place to pray. (Acts 16:13)

> As his custom was, Paul went into the synagogue, and on three Sabbath days reasoned with them from the Scriptures. (Acts 17:2)

> Every Sabbath he reasoned in the synagogue. (Acts 18:4)

Here we see Paul following the Mosaic Law, by observing the Sabbath, and keeping Jewish customs, by attending the synagogue.

Circumcision

> Paul wanted to take him [Timothy] along on the journey, so he circumcised him, for they all knew that his father was a Greek. (Acts 16:3)

Timothy's mother was a Jewess (Acts 16:1) but she had not had her son circumcised when he was a baby. Paul wanted Timothy to join him in the work but knew Timothy's testimony would not be accepted by the Jews, and so Paul circumcised him in accordance with the Mosaic Law.

Feast Days

> ... we sailed from Philippi after the feast of Unleavened Bread. (Acts 20:6)

> Paul was in a hurry to reach Jerusalem, if possible, by the day of Pentecost. (Acts 20:16)

Here we see Paul observing the special feasts of Leviticus 23. He waited in Philippi until the feast of Unleavened Bread was over; he did not sail during it. And he wanted to observe Pentecost in Jerusalem.

Other aspects of the Law

> At this the high priest Ananias ordered those standing near Paul to strike him on the mouth. Then Paul said to him, "God will strike you, you whitewashed wall! You sit there to judge me according to the law, yet you yourself violate the law by commanding that I be struck!"
> Those who were standing near Paul said, "You dare to insult God's high priest?"
> Paul replied, "Brothers, I did not realize that he was the high priest; for it is written: 'Do not speak evil about the ruler of your people.'" (Acts 23:2-5)

Here Paul shows respect for the high priest, in accordance with the Law; see Exodus 22:27-28.

> After an absence of several years, I came to Jerusalem to bring my people gifts for the poor and to present offerings. I was ceremonially clean when they found me in the temple courts doing this. (Acts 24:17-18)

Here we see that Paul was concerned about being ceremonially clean with respect to the Mosaic Law.

To sum up

We find no evidence in the Acts of the Apostles that Paul, himself, was living outside the Law of Moses. For him to take a vow in Jerusalem was not a major issue. It was not a 'compromise' for Paul. If we pay careful attention when reading Acts, we shall find that this was not the *first* vow he kept, but the *second*.

> Before he sailed, Paul had his hair cut off at Cenchrea because of a vow he had taken. (Acts 18:18)

This vow, and the later one in Acts 21 which Campbell Morgan objects to, are both in accordance with the Law of Moses (see Numbers 6:18).

The Christian Jews

During the time covered by the Acts of the Apostles, it was correct for the Christian Jews to observe the Law of Moses. If they were to witness for Christ to those Jews who did not believe that Jesus was the Christ (Messiah), the Son of God and Saviour, it was imperative that they should keep the Law. If the Christian Jews had ceased observing the Law of Moses they would have become, in the eyes of non-Christian Jews, Gentile dogs! If Christian Jews had ceased to observe the Mosaic Law, they would have lost their credibility in the eyes of non-Christian Jews, and their testimony concerning Christ would have been marred.

The Jews and the Law

What causes some confusion amongst Gentile Christians today is that in his earlier letters Paul wrote to both Jewish and Gentile Christians (see Romans, 1 & 2 Corinthians, Galatians, 1 & 2 Thessalonians). In Paul's ministry, both spoken (as recorded in Acts) and written (as recorded in his letters) he was at pains to show that the Gentiles did not need to be circumcised or to keep the Law of Moses. However, he was also at pains to let the Jewish Christians know that their salvation and righteousness was not due to their being circumcised or to their keeping the Law. It was their faith in Christ that gave them righteousness.

In Romans 4 he appealed to Abraham, who came 400 years before the Law of Moses, showing that Abraham's righteousness came through his faith, and that righteousness was credited to him before he was circumcised (Genesis 15:6; Romans 4:9-15). In doing this Paul was *not* undermining the Law of Moses, nor telling Jewish Christians that they need not observe it. He was simply pointing out the limitations of the Mosaic Law, and their misunderstanding of it, for many Jews thought their righteousness came from observing the Law. Paul, who thought that at one time, had come to learn that such righteousness was rubbish compared to the righteousness that comes through faith in Christ and which is a gift from God (Philippians 3:6-9).

The Law abolished

Although Christ fulfilled the Law on the Cross, it was not at that time abolished, as we can clearly see from the behaviour of the Apostles in the Acts. In fact, we have to wait until the end of Acts before we read anything about the abolishing of the Law.

At the end of Acts Paul arrived in Rome, called the leaders of the Jews together and tried to persuade them that Jesus was the Christ (their Messiah). Once again there was disagreement (Acts 28:17,21-24), which finally resulted in Paul uttering the judgmental prophecy from Isaiah 6 (see Acts 28:25-27), followed by the words:

> God's salvation has been sent to the Gentiles, and they will listen. (Acts 28:28)

Following this Paul spent another two years under house-arrest in Rome (Acts 28:30), during which he wrote such letters as Ephesians and Colossians. It is these letters which tell us that the Law, with commandments and ordinances, has been abolished,

> For he himself is our peace, who has made the two one and has destroyed the barrier, the dividing wall of hostility, by abolishing in his flesh the law with its commandments and regulations. (Ephesians 2:14-15)

He forgave us all our sins, having cancelled the written code, with its regulations, that was against us and that stood opposed to us; he took it away, nailing it to the cross ... Therefore do not let anyone judge you by what you eat or drink, or with regard to a religious festival, a New Moon celebration or a Sabbath day. These are a shadow of the things that were to come; the reality, however, is found in Christ. (Colossians 2:13b-17)

Also, in these latet letters, we find Paul's attitude to the Law now totally different from what it had been during the Acts period. For example, in Acts he was happy to circumcise Timothy, but after Acts circumcision by a priest was a mutilation of the flesh (e.g. see Philippians 3:2; see also verses 3-9), and had been replaced by a spiritual circumcision performed by Christ which cut off the sinful nature (Colossians 2:11).

However, we would be wrong to read this new situation – the one which appears after Acts 28:28 – back into the earlier chapters of Acts. Neither James, nor the elders, nor anyone else, had been told, during the time covered by the Acts of the Apostles, that the Law had been abolished.

James and the elders were therefore right to ask Paul to take the vow, and Paul did not compromise himself by doing so. During Acts he observed the Law of Moses and told all Jews everywhere to do the same. After Acts, he did not observe the Law of Moses, and told the Christian Jews that neither did they need to observe it. However, we are wrong to read the revelation God gave after Acts back into Acts.

Part 3

Comments and Queries about the Jewish Letters

16 James addressed his letter "To all God's people: everywhere." True or false?

The words above are the first words of the letter of James in the *Good News Bible*. It is how the translators of that version render the start of that epistle, but in doing so they hide from uninformed readers something very significant, and important.

To understand any letter we read, whether it be one written today in the 21st Century or one written 2,000 years ago in the 1st Century, we must know to whom it is addressed. From what we read in the *Good News Bible* it seems that James addressed his letter to each and every Christian, to every type of believer; but is that actually the case? Below is a list of how several translations render those words from the first verse of James.

- To the twelve tribes scattered amongst the nations (NIV)
- To the twelve tribes which are scattered abroad. (KJV)
- To the twelve tribes who are dispersed abroad. (NASV)
- To the twelve tribes dispersed throughout the world. (REB)
- To the twelve tribes in the Dispersion. (Moffatt)
- To the Twelve Tribes who are in the dispersion. (Young's Literal Translation)
- To the twelve tribes which [are] in the dispersion. (Interlinear Greek-English NT)

There are two significant aspects in these words:

1. the twelve tribes, and
2. scattered or dispersed.

The word translated 'scattered' or 'dispersed' is the Greek *diaspora*, which was a technical term:

... used of the Jews who, from time to time, had been scattered among the Gentiles. (Vine's *Expository Dictionary of New Testament Words*)

Thus James does **not** address his letter generally to "all God's people", but rather specifically to Jewish Christians. However, he was not concerned with those Jewish Christians who lived in Jerusalem, Judea and Galilee. After all, if they wanted words and wisdom from James they could, with relative ease, go up to Jerusalem and see him. No! James was concerned about the Jewish Christians who were scattered throughout the Roman Empire and elsewhere.

Does this matter?

Some may question whether this really matters because, as Paul stated, "All Scripture is God-breathed and is useful for teaching, rebuking, correcting and training in righteousness, so that the man of God may be thoroughly equipped for every good work," (2 Timothy 3:16-17).

Certainly there is much that 21st Century Gentile Christians can learn from the letter of James. His words about being doers and not merely listeners and of showing our faith by our deeds are very relevant. What he wrote about the wrongs of favouritism and the evils of the tongue apply equally to Jewish or Gentile Christians of all ages. We can learn much from what he wrote about the 'two kinds of wisdom' at the end of chapter 3, but what about the wisdom in the opening chapter? And the promise that if anyone lacks wisdom all he need do is ask and wisdom **will** be given? Sadly, I have seen a number of Christians who, having asked for wisdom, have then made some very unwise decisions.

The background to James

One of James' concerns was the trials, tribulations and testing being experienced by the Jewish Christians of the dispersion in those early days following Christ's ascension (James 1:2-4,13; 5:10). This persecution was not at the hands of the Romans (that came later under Caesar Nero), but came from the Jewish leadership, as we see in such places as Acts 5:18,40 and 17:5-7, for example.

James was possibly the first New Testament document to have been written, and almost certainly the first letter. We note that there is not one mention in the letter of the word 'Gentile' and every reference to 'the world' is derogatory (James 1:27; 2:5; 3:6; 4:4). This is one of the reasons why some have suggested James was written early in Acts, even before Peter was sent to Cornelius (Acts 10). For the struggling, persecuted Jewish Christians of the Dispersion to have received a letter from the brother of Jesus would have been a source of great comfort and encouragement. But why were they suffering? Who was persecuting them?

Christ's Promise

> "But before all this, they will lay hands on you and persecute you. They will deliver you to synagogues and prisons, and you will be brought before kings and governors, and all on account of my name. This will result in your being witnesses to them. But make up your mind not to worry beforehand how you will defend yourselves. For I will give you words and wisdom that none of your adversaries will be able to resist or contradict. You will be betrayed even by parents, brothers, relatives and friends, and they will put some of you to death." (Luke 21:12-16)

From these words of our Saviour it seems that they were persecuted not only by the secular and religious authorities, but also by their own families and friends, and in their own synagogues. Why would they be persecuted? Verse 17 states, "all men will hate you *because of me*". These Jewish Christians were being persecuted quite simply because they were Christians, because they believed Jesus to be the Son of God, the Christ (Messiah).

If we find this difficult to accept we need only read the Acts of the Apostles and see the persecution there. Peter and John ran into trouble with the high priest, the rulers and elders, the teachers of the Law, for preaching Christ and healing in His name (Acts 4:1-21; 5:17-42). Paul, too, suffered great rebuffs from certain synagogues when he explained that Jesus was the Christ, the Son of God. He was argued against, imprisoned, beaten, and stoned.

However, Christ promised that when they were in such situations they "should not worry beforehand" as to how they were going to defend themselves because He would give them "words and *wisdom*" that none of their adversaries would be able to answer. We see this in operation with a number of the Jewish Christians in Acts. For example:

- Peter and John; Acts 5:13
- Stephen: Acts 6:8-10
- Paul: Acts 9:20-22

James' Reminder

The first thing James did in his letter to the persecuted Jewish Christians of the Dispersion was to remind them of this promise of wisdom (i.e. the one Jesus gave in Luke 21:12-16).

> "But before all this, they will seize you and persecute you. They will hand you over to synagogues and put you in prison, and you will be brought before kings and governors, and all on account of my name. And so you will bear testimony to me. But make up your mind not to worry beforehand how you will defend yourselves. For I will give you words and *wisdom* that none of your adversaries will be able to resist or contradict. You will be betrayed even by parents, brothers and sisters, relatives and friends, and they will put some of you to death.

They need not worry beforehand how to defend themselves and answer people. Words and wisdom would be given them. There is no doubt about this: "it *will* be given" (James 1:5). There are no "ifs and buts"; there is no "may". It "will" be given, in accordance with Christ's promise.

But what about us?

Christ's promise in Luke 21 was not given to Gentile Christians of the 1st century and certainly it would be wrong of 21st Century Gentile Christians to usurp it. However, there is a prayer for wisdom which is appropriate for us. Paul wrote Ephesians after the end of the Acts period. There we read:

> I keep asking that the God of our Lord Jesus Christ, the glorious Father, may give you the Spirit of wisdom and revelation, so that you may know him better. (Ephesians 1:17)

This is the prayer that Paul kept offering on behalf of the Christians to whom he wrote, both Jewish and Gentile. However, there are two things to note that are significantly different from what James wrote in 1:5.

1) Firstly, note that Paul does not state that the wisdom "will" be given, but asks that it "may" be given. Thus if we pray for wisdom there is no guarantee that God will grant it to us.
2) Secondly, note that the wisdom in the prayer of Ephesians 1:17 is not so that we can confound our adversaries with wise words. Rather it is so that we may have greater knowledge and understanding of our heavenly Father.

17 Confession is a 'must' for forgiveness True or false?

In some services in the Anglican Church a 'Prayer for Forgiveness' is offered, after which I am extremely reluctant to say 'Amen'.

> **Prayer for Forgiveness**
> God our Father, you made us and you love us. We know that you forgive us when we are sorry for what we have done; we thank you for your loving kindness, and ask you to help us to do better for you, and for Jesus Christ our Lord, who showed us your love. Amen.

Forgiveness by Confession

In the Catholic tradition there are seven sacraments and to the Catholic, a sacrament is a means to grace and hence forgiveness. One of these sacraments is confession. Sins that are confessed are forgiven; sins that are not confessed are not forgiven unless they are covered by another sacrament, such as participation in the Mass.

In the past (and this is probably still so today) the majority of Catholics spent little time in confession. However, a person with a sensitive conscience (or who is well aware just how far short humans fall in thought, as well as in word and deed) may spend an inordinate amount of time in confession. Such a person was Martin Luther, who spent many hours each day in confession. Eventually Luther was to conclude that there must be a different way of securing forgiveness and, of course, he eventually discovered what the Bible taught: "the just shall live by faith alone". In other words, forgiveness is secured, and righteousness imputed, when people believe that Christ died for their sins.

General Confession

The idea that sins need to be confessed is still quite common amongst non-Catholic Christians. The *General Confession* of the Church of

England, in fact, encourages it. However, it is a 'general' confession and individual sins need not be confessed. Sins are confessed in categories: thought, word, and deed; through negligence and weakness, as well as being deliberate. Then, after this general confession, the congregation ask for forgiveness for what is past; but what about future sins? Are they not forgiven? What if someone should die in a car accident before next Sunday? Will they be eternally condemned because of unconfessed (and thus unforgiven) sins? Before answering this question we need to look at another.

> **The General Confession**
> Almighty God, our heavenly Father, we have sinned against you and against our fellow men, in thought and word and deed, through negligence, through weakness, through our own deliberate fault. We are truly sorry and repent of all our sins, For the sake of your Son Jesus Christ, who died for us, forgive us all that is past; and grant us that we may serve you in newness of life to the glory of your name, Amen.

Specific Confession

There are, even in Bible teaching evangelical circles, some Christians who, while firmly believing that Christ died for their sins, believe also that they must confess each individual sin for it to be forgiven. This view is based upon a verse in one of John's letters but, before turning to that, we ought perhaps to consider the following questions.

What about the sins we do that we forget about? What about those sins we do that we are not aware of? A person may offend someone and not be conscious of the offence, and so does not confess it. Does that mean that that person is eternally condemned because they have committed a sin that they have forgotten or were unaware of? I know in my early years of being a Christian I committed many sins, quite simply because I did not know all the things that the Bible said were wrong! We are told "it is by grace you have been saved, through *faith* [not through confession]" (Ephesians 2:8).

The Gospel of Salvation

One of the clearest statements concerning the gospel of salvation is found in 1 Corinthians 15:3-4. Having spoken of that gospel in verse 2, Paul goes on to say:

> For what I received I passed on to you as of first importance: that Christ died for our sins according to the Scriptures, that he was buried, that he was raised on the third day according to the Scriptures.

And at the end of Romans 4 Paul makes it clear that we have forgiveness, with the accompanying righteousness and justification, through Christ dying for our sins and being raised to life.

> The words "it was credited to him" were written not for him alone, but also for us, to whom God will credit righteousness - for us who believe in him who raised Jesus our Lord from the dead. He was delivered over to death for our sins and was raised to life for our justification. (Romans 4:23-25)

Thus the first step in being saved is that we acknowledge that we are sinners. Acknowledging that we are sinners not only recognises that we have committed sins in the past *but* also that we will continue to do so in the future, albeit to a lesser extent. This is *the* confession that we all need to make.

The next step is to accept that Christ died for those sins (past, present and future) and that He was raised from the dead as evidence that His sacrifice had been accepted, and so we know we are justified in God's eyes.

Confession for forgiveness

If this be the case, why does John write ...

If we confess our sins, he is faithful and just and will forgive us our sins and purify us from all unrighteousness. (1 John 1:9)

What exactly does John mean here? He seems to be going not only against all that Paul has written, but also against what he himself wrote in such places as John 3:16. There we read, "For God so loved the world that he gave his one and only Son, that whoever believes in him shall not perish but have eternal life."

We need to appreciate that John wrote during the period of time covered by the Acts of the Apostles, and that he wrote primarily for Jewish Christians. During that time there were many miracles. These were signs to the people of Israel, to signify to them that Jesus was the Christ (Messiah), the Son of God (see John 20:30-31). Most of these miracles were blessings, but some were judgments. If, for example, a Jewish Christian committed certain sins he could be struck dead, as Ananias and Sapphira were (Acts 5:1-11), or struck with illness, as some of the Corinthian Christians were (1 Corinthians 11:27-30). If a Jewish Christian at that time had committed some sin and was suffering from a judgmental illness, what could he do about it? The letter of James, also written during the time covered by the Acts of the Apostles, and also written to Jewish Christians, supplies the answer.

> Is any one of you sick? He should call the elders of the church to pray over him and anoint him with oil in the name of the Lord. And the prayer offered in faith will make the sick person well; the Lord will raise him up. If he has sinned, he will be forgiven. Therefore *confess your sins* to each other and pray for each other *so that* you may be healed. The prayer of a righteous man is powerful and effective. (James 5:14-16)[15]

Here we read that those Jewish Christians who had committed certain sins, and who had been struck with a judgmental illness, could secure forgiveness for healing. However, they needed to *confess* those sins.

---

[15] For a more detailed treatment of this passage see *James: His life and letter* by Michael Penny, published by The Open Bible Trust.

"Confess your sins ... so that you may be healed" is what James wrote. Please note: this is confession and forgiveness for *healing*; it is **not** forgiveness for salvation and eternal life.

It appears to be the same in John's letter, for John goes on to mention the need of prayer for people who might commit such sins.

> If anyone sees his brother commit a sin that does not lead to death, he should pray and God will give him life. I refer to those whose sin does not lead to death. There is a sin that leads to death. I am not saying that he should pray about that. All wrongdoing is sin, and there is sin that does not lead to death. (1 John 5:16-17)[16]

Note that John also speaks of "the sin that leads to death": ones similar to those committed by Ananias and Sapphira, Herod, and also some of the Corinthian Christians; see Acts 5:1-10; 12:19-22; 1 Corinthians 11:27-30.

What can be done?

So what can I do at such services? In the *Prayer for Forgiveness* it would be so simple to change

> We know that you forgive us when we are sorry for what we have done...

to

> We know that you have forgiven us and we are sorry for what we have done.

And in the *General Confession* one could change

---

[16] For a more detailed consideration of 1 John 1:9 and 5:16, as well as James 5:15, see chapters 34,35 & 36 of Michael Penny's *40 Problem Passages*, available from the Open Bible Trust.

We are truly sorry and repent of all our sins, For the sake of your Son Jesus Christ, who died for us, forgive us all that is past; and grant us that we may serve you in newness of life to the glory of your name ...

to

We are truly sorry and repent of all our sins. For the sake of your Son Jesus Christ, who died for us, you have forgiven us all our sins. Grant that we may serve you in newness of life to the glory of your name.

There is certainly *nothing* wrong with apologising to the person we have sinned against, and when we sin, not only do we offend other human beings, we also offend our loving heavenly Father, and can grieve the Holy Spirit with whom we are sealed (Ephesians 4:30). Thus every sin may warrant two apologies. Whether our human brother or sister will forgive or not may be open to question. However, if we believe that Christ died for our sins, our heavenly Father has already done so.

18 Whoever is born of God does not sin
True or false?

There are a couple of verses in John's first letter which, in some translations, seem to teach that those who are Christians do not sin, and that, if someone does sin, then they do not know God.

> Whosoever abideth in him sinneth not: whoever sinneth hath not seen him, neither known him. (1 John 3:6; *KJV*)
> Whoever abides in him does not sin. Whoever sins has neither seen him nor known him. (1 John 3:6; *NJKV*)

> Whoever is born of God doth not commit sin; for his seed remaineth in him: and he cannot sin, because he nis born of God. (1 John 3:9; *KJV*)
> Whoever has been born of God does not sin, for his seed remains in him; and he cannot sin, because he has been born of God. (1 John 3:9; *NKJV*)

> We know that whosoever is born of God sinneth not. (1 John 5:18; *KJV*)
> We know that whoever is born of God does not sin. (1 John 5:18; *NKJV*)

Such verses as these have caused some people to doubt the sincerity of either their own faith in Christ, or the faith of others. All of us are aware that even after we have come to believe in the Lord Jesus Christ we still, at times, sin. We are acutely aware of the truth that "all have sinned and fall short of the glory of God" (Romans 3:23). That was true of us before we had faith and it continues to be true afterwards so ... does that mean we do not know God? That we are not born of God? That we are not His children?

Peter, Paul and Barnabas

When we read through the Scriptures we see that some of the leading Christians had failings. For example: Paul and Barnabas argued so sharply over John Mark that they had to go their separate ways (Acts 15:36-41). And Peter, when he visited the church in Antioch, refused to eat with Gentile Christians and caused much dissension (Galatians 2:11-14). Does that mean that Peter and Paul and Barnabas had not seen God and did not know Him? Certainly not!

And many, many years after he had become a Christian, the Apostle Paul wrote:

> For I have the desire to do what is good, but cannot carry it out. For what I do is not the good I want to do; no, the evil I do not want to do – this I keep on doing. (Romans 7:18–19)

So Paul, clearly a mature Christian, found himself committing sins both of commission (doing wrong) and omission (not doing good). Earlier in this first letter John wrote:

> If we say that we have no sin, we deceive ourselves, and the truth is not in us. (1 John 1:8; *KJV*)

> If we claim to be without sin, we deceive ourselves and the truth is not in us. (1 John 1:8; *NIV*)

If John states this in chapter 1, what does he mean in chapters 3 and 5?

Continue in sin

The problem is solved if we consider other translations. For example:

- No one who lives in him keeps on sinning. No one who continues to sin has either seen him or known him. (1 John 3:6; *NIV*)
- No one who abides in him keeps on sinning; no one who keeps on sinning has either seen him or known him. (1 John 3:6; *ESV*)

- No one who is born of God will continue to sin, because God's seed remains in him; he cannot go on sinning, because he has been born of God. (1 John 3:9; *NIV*)
- No one born of God makes a practice of sinning, for God's seed abides in him, and he cannot keep on sinning because he has been born of God. (1 John 3:9; *ESV*)

- We know that anyone born of God does not continue to sin. (1 John 5:18; *NIV*)
- We know that everyone who has been born of God does not keep on sinning. (1 John 5:18; *ESV*)

Here, in these translations, we have a different slant: it is not that believers never sin, but that they do not continually sin; they do not make a practice of sin; they do not keep repeating the same mistake. The *Amplified Bible*, in its extended paraphrase, makes this very clear.

> No one who abides in Him [who lives and remains in communion with and in obedience to Him—deliberately, knowingly, and habitually] commits (practices) sin. No one who [habitually] sins has either seen *or* known Him [recognized, perceived, or understood Him, or has had an experiential acquaintance with Him]. (1 John 3:6)

> No one born (begotten) of God [deliberately and knowingly] habitually practices sin, for God's nature abides in him - His principle of life, the divine sperm, remains permanently within him - and he cannot practice sinning because he is born (begotten) of God. (1 John 3:9)

> We know [absolutely] that anyone born of God does not [deliberately and knowingly] practice committing sin. (1 John 5:18)

Paul did not practice sin; he did not regularly sin; but, even after twenty or more years of being a believer, he could find himself, at times, not doing the good he wanted to do but, instead, the evil he did ***not*** want to do. However, throughout all this his 'desire' was to do the right and good (Romans 7:18). So what would cause people like Peter and Paul to sin?

Peter, in Antioch, was pressurised by a group of Jewish Christians from Jerusalem. The result was he separated himself from the Gentile believers because they were not circumcised, an event which took place at the end of Acts 14 (or start of Acts 15) when Paul was in Antioch and it is recorded for us in Galatians 2:11-21. However, a little later at the Jerusalem Council in Acts 15:6-21, he totally supported Paul and the teaching that Gentiles did not need to be circumcised to be saved (Acts 15:6-11). He did not continue in the sin.

Whatever the problem was with John Mark, it caused Paul and Barnabas to separate. However, that situation did not continue. The problem was put right as we read that Mark was later in Rome with Paul (Colossians 4:10) and, just before he was martyred, Paul wanted to see Mark because he was "helpful" in Paul's ministry (2 Timothy 4:11).

Caught in a sin

It would seem, then, that these were isolated incidents which were somehow or other put right: maybe by the individuals themselves, or possibly with the help of others. And such an example of sin is what Paul wrote about in Galatians 6:1:

> Brother, if someone is caught in a sin, you who are spiritual should restore him gently. But watch yourself, or you also may be tempted.

Peter was 'caught' in a situation which caused him to sin when he denied the Lord three times, but he never denied Him again. Under pressure from the 'circumcision group' when they arrived in Antioch, Peter stopped eating with Gentiles. Here he was 'caught' again, in a different type of sin, and Paul restored him (Galatians 2:11-16).
In Philippi a situation arose which concerned Paul.

> I plead with Euodia and I plead with Syntyche to agree with each other in the Lord. Yes, and I ask you, loyal yokefellow, help these women who have contended at my side in the cause of the gospel, along with Clement and the rest of my fellow-workers, whose names are in the book of life. (Philippians 4:2-3)

Whatever it was that caused the Christian women to fall out, Paul wanted his friend to help them.

We all have different personalities, with different strengths and weaknesses. As well as being 'caught' by circumstances and pressures, and thus stumbling and falling on the odd occasion, we may be 'caught' by our personal make-up. Some people are naturally more patient than others; some more placid. Those of us who are naturally less patient and placid have a greater tendency towards irritability and anger, and thus we may 'continue' in that sin for some time. The issue is ... what is the 'desire' of one's heart? Paul's desire was to do the good (Romans 7:18). Do we want to do the good, change and so try to control that sin, or are we content just to carry on with the sin and 'practice' it?

What about us ... and others?

It is so easy for us, in certain situations and under pressure from others, to say or do something wrong. Let us make a determined effort to learn from that experience and ensure that we avoid such a situation in the future. And let us prayerfully, calling on God's help, resist such pressure another time. We need to realise that we are sealed with His Holy Spirit, who can empower us (Ephesians 3:14-19). However, we also need to realise that what we say or do can "grieve the Holy Spirit" with whom we are sealed (Ephesians 4:30).

On the other hand, if we see a brother or sister sin, we should not be judgmental of them, but neither should we ignore the situation. Our duty is to graciously point out the failing and gently restore them, all in a spirit of humility. However, that is not an easy thing to do. It is so much easier to say nothing and hope they will not do it again but, if they do sin again ... then we must share some of the responsibility.

Part 4

Comments and Queries about Paul's Earlier Letters

19 Paul was against marriage
True or false?

Over the years I have read and heard many comments about Paul and women and marriage. Apparently, some suggest, he was anti-women and anti-marriage. However, if we read **all** of each letter Paul wrote, we find that Paul had great regard and high respect for women, often mentioning them, praising them, and thanking them.

The view that he was *anti-marriage* is built upon one chapter of the letter he wrote to the Corinthians. Please read 1 Corinthians 7 and note the following:

> Now for the matters you wrote about: It is good for a man not to marry. But since there is so much immorality, each man should have his own wife, and each woman her own husband ... I wish that all men were as I am. But each man has his own gift from God; one has this gift, another has that.
>
> Now to the unmarried and the widows I say: It is good for them to stay unmarried, as I am. But if they cannot control themselves, they should marry, for it is better to marry than to burn with passion. (1 Corinthians 7:1-9)

Best not to marry

Here it seems that Paul is saying that the only reason for marriage is the inability of people to "control themselves", thus enabling them to cope and not be tempted by all the sexual immorality that abounded in Corinth. However, the passage states, it was best to stay unmarried, as Paul was.

> Now about virgins ... Because of the present crisis, I think that it is good for you to remain as you are. Are you married? Do not seek a divorce. Are you unmarried? Do not look for a wife ... But those who marry will face many troubles in this life, and I want to spare you this. What I mean, brothers, is that the time is

short. From now on those who have wives should live as if they had none. (1 Corinthians 7:25-29)

Here again, while telling married people *not* to separate, he also tells the unmarried it is best *not* to get married. Not only that, he tells them that if they do get married, they will face many troubles. Furthermore those who are married and have wives "should live as if they had none": i.e. they should refrain from intimacy.

> I would like you to be free from concern. An unmarried man is concerned about the Lord's affairs - how he can please the Lord. But a married man is concerned about the affairs of this world - how he can please his wife - and his interests are divided. An unmarried woman or virgin is concerned about the Lord's affairs: her aim is to be devoted to the Lord in both body and spirit. But a married woman is concerned about the affairs of this world - how she can please her husband. I am saying this for your own good, not to restrict you, but that you may live in a right way in undivided devotion to the Lord. (1 Corinthians 7:32-35)

Better to be single

Here, again, the single person is seen to be better able to serve the Lord than the married one, but is that the case today? Was that so when Paul wrote? Has something changed?

> If anyone thinks he is acting improperly towards the virgin he is engaged to, and if she is getting on in years and he feels he ought to marry, he should do as he wants. He is not sinning. They should get married. But the man who has settled the matter in his own mind, who is under no compulsion but has control over his own will, and who has made up his mind not to marry the virgin - this man also does the right thing. So then, he who marries the virgin does right, but he who does not marry her does even better.

A woman is bound to her husband as long as he lives. But if her husband dies, she is free to marry anyone she wishes, but he must belong to the Lord. In my judgment, she is happier if she stays as she is - and I think that I too have the Spirit of God. (1 Corinthians 7:36-40)

Again the reason for marriage is the inability to control sexual desire, and furthermore the widow is told she would be happier if she remained unmarried, rather than remarry. All this would suggest that the criticism that Paul was against marriage has some merit, and this is the line taken, for example, by such writers as Don Williams in *The Apostle Paul & Women in the Church*. On page 58 he writes:

Paul argues, not from the tradition of Jesus, but from his own gift and authority, for celibacy (7:7,25). Since the Christian lives in the crisis time between the first and second coming of Christ, where time is short, and the form of the world is passing away (7:26,29,31), his best position is the freedom of the single state.

If, however, he is married he should not seek to be free. If single, he should not seek marriage (7:27). Marriage, while not sinful (7:28), is not expedient.

But is Williams[17] correct in his understanding that "the present crisis" spans the years between Christ's first and second comings? The word "present" implies that the crisis is not long-term, yet Williams sees it as occupying the two thousand years or more!

---

[17] In this chapter I have disagreed with a fellow Christian, Don Williams, whom I respect very much (and a considerable amount of what is in his book is good and edifying). However, his idea that the "present crisis", the "last days", and similar terms, refer to the period between the Lord's first and second comings is a common view held by a number of Christians, but it is a view I cannot share. For a fuller explanation of the purpose of the period of time covered by the Acts of the Apostles, and how it could have led up to Christ's return, please see *Approaching the Bible* (OBT).

The present crisis

The view that "present" implies a short-term, immediate problem is further reinforced by Paul saying that "the time is short" (v 29) and that "this world in its present form is passing away". If such expressions refer to the two thousand plus years between the Lord's first and second comings, then they are very misleading.

However, the biggest argument against Williams' position comes from the pen of the Apostle Paul himself. Some ten to twenty years after writing to the Corinthians Paul wrote to Timothy, and there he told him:

> So I counsel younger widows to marry, to have children, to manage their homes and to give the enemy no opportunity for slander. (1 Timothy 5:14)

If all that Williams says about the crisis occupying the years between Christ's first and second coming is valid, why did Paul later counsel the younger widows to marry?

Elsewhere[18] I have dealt with the issue of the *possibility* of Christ's second coming following on closely from His first. Peter makes this very clear at the start of the Acts of the Apostles.

> "Now, brothers, I know that you acted in ignorance, as did your leaders. But this is how God fulfilled what he had foretold through all the prophets, saying that his Christ would suffer. Repent, then, and turn to God, so that your sins may be wiped out, that times of refreshing may come from the Lord, and that he may send the Christ, who has been appointed for you - even Jesus. He must remain in heaven until the time comes for God to restore everything, as he promised long ago through his holy prophets." (Acts 3:17-21)

---

[18] See chapter 21 of *True or False? Questions and Queries about Christianity* – details on page 176.

Here Peter called upon the people of Israel to repent and turn to God. He asked them to repent:

> so that ... your sins may be wiped out;
> so that ... the times of refreshing may come from the Lord;
>   and
> so that ... He [God] may send the Christ, who has been appointed for you - even Jesus.

Peter stated that the return of Christ, at that time, was dependent upon the repentance of the people of Israel. Christ was to remain in heaven until the time came for God to restore everything. Restoration of everything was to start with the restoration of the people of Israel (Acts 1:6), and their restoration depended upon their repentance.

A great distress

However, if the people of Israel did, at that time, repent and turn to Christ, the prophetic scenario of Matthew 24 would have to run its course before He returned. That would include such events as:

- wars and rumours of wars;
- nation against nation;
- kingdom against kingdom;
- famines and earthquakes;
- persecution and death;
- increase in wickedness.

All this culminates with the abomination of desolation set up in the temple in Jerusalem and those in Judea fleeing into the mountains. This time is described by the Lord as a time of "great *distress*, unequalled from the beginning of the world until now – and never to be equalled again" (Matthew 24:21). During such a time our Lord Jesus Christ said:

> "How dreadful it will be in those days for pregnant women and nursing mothers!" (Matthew 24:19)

And all this could have happened in Paul's day if the Jewish nation had repented. Thus, speaking of the same era as Matthew 24, the Apostle Paul wrote:

- It is good for a man not to marry.
- It is good for them to stay unmarried, as I am.
- Virgins ... Because of the present crisis, I think that it is good for you to remain as you are.
- Are you unmarried? Do not look for a wife.
- But those who marry will face many troubles in this life, and I want to spare you this.
- What I mean, brothers, is that the time is short.
- From now on those who have wives should live as if they had none.

In other words, these are not the words of a person who is anti-marriage *per se*.

Paul's advice to those considering marriage is that they should remain unmarried; not because marriage is in any sense wrong, but rather because he would spare them anxiety. As Bruce puts it, "The conflict of interest and cares to which Christians with family responsibilities are ordinarily subject is intensified in times of 'distress' and Paul wants his readers to be free from such worries." There is no disdain of marriage as such, but in the last times, to be married is harder than to be single and Paul has a pastoral concern here both for the individuals concerned and for the church as a whole.

(Mary Evans, p 72, *Woman in the Bible*)

Don Williams states Paul is *not* following in the tradition of Jesus, but if we look closely we will find that Paul most certainly is. In 1 Corinthians 7, Paul is echoing what Christ said in Matthew 24: Paul is building upon and expanding what the Lord Jesus Christ said in Matthew 24:19. Here we have a caring apostle[19] who wishes to spare married couples the sorrow and heartache of seeing their children go through the worst crisis (great tribulation, *KJV*) the world will ever see. However, that crisis did not come about. Although individual Jews did accept Jesus as their Messiah (Christ) and Saviour, the nation in general, and the leadership in particular, did not. Thus at the end of Acts we read the final pronouncement of Isaiah's judgmental prophecy upon Israel.

> "Go to this people and say, 'You will be ever hearing but never understanding; you will be ever seeing but never perceiving.'
> For this people's heart has become calloused; they hardly hear with their ears, and they have closed their eyes. Otherwise they might see with their eyes, hear with their ears, understand with their hearts and turn, and I would heal them."
> (Act 28:26-27)

That nation, at that time, lost its prime position as a special nation before God and "God's salvation has been sent to the Gentiles" (Acts 28:28).

Israel had not repented and so the conditions needed for the early return of Christ were not met, and that great event is still future. That meant that the great distress, which precedes His second coming, did not come about. The "present crisis" which Paul wrote of in 1 Corinthians ended. The time before Christ was to return may have been 'short' when Paul wrote Corinthians, but that was no longer the case at the end of Acts. And the world in its present form was no longer passing away; it was carrying on. Thus life had to get back to normal, and what is more normal than getting married and having children?

As a result of this change, a little while after the words of Acts 28:25-28 were written, Paul wrote to Timothy and in that letter he counselled the widows to marry ***and*** to have children.

---

[19] For more on Paul and women see *Woman to Woman* compiled and edited by Sylvia Penny, published by the Open Bible Trust; and note especially section 7 *The Apostle Paul and Women.*

> So I counsel younger widows to marry, to have children, to manage their homes and to give the enemy no opportunity for slander. (1 Timothy 5:14)

Of course, sometime in the future, as we approach those days when Christ returns and we see *all* the events of Matthew 24 beginning to unfold, then Paul's words in 1 Corinthians 7 may, yet again, be sensible advice to follow.

20 Sinning more increases grace True or false?

Some parts of Paul's earlier letters are not easy to understand. This is because they were written during the period covered by the Acts of the Apostles and sent to churches which were a mixture of Jews and Gentiles. At that time the Jewish Christian took precedence (Romans 1:16; 2:9-10). At that time there was an advantage in being a Jew (Romans 3:1-2), and because they were the people who had the Scriptures we see that, within the Christendom of the period of time covered by the Acts of the Apostles, all the evangelists and leaders were Jews.

Romans 1:16
For I am not ashamed of the gospel, because it is the power of God that brings salvation to everyone who believes: *first to the Jew*, then to the Gentile.
Romans 2:9-10
There will be trouble and distress for every human being who does evil: *first for the Jew*, then for the Gentile; but glory, honour and peace *for everyone who does good: first* for the Jew, then for the Gentile.
Romans 3:1-2
What advantage, then, is there in being a Jew, or what value is there in circumcision? *Much in every way!* First of all, the Jews have been entrusted with the very words of God.

While parts of those earlier letters deal with issues that were common to both groups, others were specifically addressed to Jewish Christians, while yet other parts dealt with issues that affected the Gentiles. In certain places this is obvious. For example, 1 Corinthians 10:1-2 starts off the Jewish section of 1 Corinthians.

> For I do not want you to be ignorant of the fact, brothers, that *our forefathers* were all under the cloud and that they all passed through the sea. *They were all baptized into Moses* in the cloud and in the sea. (1 Corinthians 10:1-2)

This Jewish section continues to the end of chapter 11. Then chapter 12:1-2 commences a section aimed at the Gentile Christians.

Now about spiritual gifts, brothers, I do not want you to be ignorant. You know that when *you were pagans*, somehow or other you were influenced and led astray to mute idols. (1 Corinthians 12:1-2)

However, in some other places it is not obvious to whom Paul was addressing his comments, or as to whether the issue he was dealing with was a problem for Jewish Christians or Gentile ones. A case in point is Romans 6:1, where we read:

What shall we say, then? Shall we go on sinning so that grace may increase? *(NIV)*

What shall we say then? Shall we continue in sin, that grace may abound? *(KJV)*

Distorted glory

From a number of passages in Romans it seems that the Roman Christians, or a section of them, had a distorted view of glory. For example:

Someone might argue, "If my falsehood enhances God's truthfulness and so increases his glory, why am I still condemned as a sinner?" Why not say - as we are being slanderously reported as saying and as some claim that we say - "Let us do evil that good may result"? Their condemnation is deserved. (Romans 3:8)

Here, it seems that some of the Roman Christians had concluded that telling lies was perfectly acceptable, and they should not be condemned as sinners for doing so. Their falsehoods enhanced God's truthfulness and that would bring greater glory to God ... or so they thought! Man is such a sinner and God is so holy; our lying exaggerates the difference between God and man and so enhances God's glory! Some were even trying to attribute such a view to Paul, by claiming that his attitude was

"Let us do evil that good may abound" (a view which Paul roundly condemned). But how could any Christian come to such a view?

Distorted grace

Christians are indeed saved by grace through faith and not by works. Because of the all-sufficiency of Christ's sacrifice for sin we are assured forgiveness of *all* our sins. Paul had just emphasised this in Romans 5.

> You see, at just the right time, when we were still powerless, Christ died for the ungodly ... But God demonstrates his own love for us in this: While we were still sinners, Christ died for us ... For if, when we were God's enemies, we were reconciled to him through the death of his Son, how much more, having been reconciled, shall we be saved through his life! (Romans 5:6,8,10)

Thus Christ died for ungodly sinners who were His enemies. What grace! And how can we magnify this grace? By sinning more? That is what some of the Roman Christians thought, but Paul again roundly condemns such an attitude (Romans 6:2).

Jewish or Gentile Christians?

It is hard to imagine any Jewish Christians having such a low regard for God's glory and grace, or indeed such a lax attitude towards immorality. After all, they had the Scriptures, the very Word of God, and they revered them and tried to live by what they taught about God and His commandments.

Thus this seems to have been a problem for the Gentile Christians in Rome. However, why hadn't it been dealt with by the Jewish Christian leaders in the church at Rome? The answer could well be that the Jewish Christians were no longer around.

> After this, Paul left Athens and went to Corinth. There he met a Jew named Aquila, a native of Pontus, who had recently come

from Italy with his wife Priscilla, because Claudius had ordered all the Jews to leave Rome. (Acts 18:1-2)

Claudius, one of the best Caesars of his time, respected religious freedom. At that time Christianity was considered by the Romans to be a branch of Judaism, but there was much friction between the Christian Jews (who were preaching the gospel and gaining converts, both Jewish ones and Gentile ones) and the non-Christian Jews. The problems arising from this evangelising were such that Claudius expelled all the Jews, including the Christian ones.

Alone and leaderless

This left the Christian Gentiles in Rome alone and leaderless. Previously these Gentiles would have been pagans, worshipping in the pagan temples. Although many would have understood and believed the gospel message of salvation by grace through faith and not by works, they would not have fully understood all the ramifications and implications of this.

Many would have retained, subconsciously, some of their paganism. Both the Roman and Greek gods committed quite extraordinary, immoral acts, and in some of the pagan temples the adherents also performed these acts, which were viewed as acts of worship, for the worshippers were seen as mimicking their gods. (The Gentile Christians of Corinth had a similar problem, hence Paul writing to them in 1 Corinthians 6:15-16.)

The type of sin that the Roman Christians were involved in is spelled out in Romans 13:13, where Paul wrote:

> Let us behave decently, as in the daytime, not in orgies and drunkenness, not in sexual immorality and debauchery, not in dissension and jealousy. Rather, clothe yourselves with the Lord Jesus Christ, and do not think about how to gratify the desires of the sinful nature. (Romans 13:13-14)

Because of the temptations from the society around them, because they were young in the faith, because they had no leadership, some of the Gentile Christians from Rome slipped into, or returned to, the pagan practices. However, they also tried to justify themselves by saying such behaviour actually glorified God by magnifying His grace and forgiveness. Their attitude was, as God loves us and forgives us, the more we sin the more we show just how great His love and forgiveness are!

Application

We rejoice knowing that we have a wonderful, loving heavenly Father who has forgiven us all our sins (Colossians 1:14; 2:13). The all-sufficiency of Christ's sacrifice for sin means that not only are past (and present) sins forgiven, but so too are future ones. The fact that this is guaranteed by grace (Romans 4:16; 2 Corinthians 1:22; 5:5; Ephesians 1:14), does not give us license to live as *we* like, because we know that our sins grieve Him (Ephesians 4:30).

> Do not let any unwholesome talk come out of your mouths, but only what is helpful for building others up according to their needs, that it may benefit those who listen. And do not grieve the Holy Spirit of God, with whom you were sealed for the day of redemption. Get rid of all bitterness, rage and anger, brawling and slander, along with every form of malice. Be kind and compassionate to one another, forgiving each other, just as in Christ God forgave you. (Ephesians 4:29-32)

Rather, it gives us the liberty to live as *He* wishes us to live and if, on occasion, we slip or fall, or act out of character, then we have the security net of grace to catch us and restore us.

> What good is it, my brothers, if a man claims to have faith but has no deeds? Can such faith save him? (James 2:14)

The Jews of the dispersion, to whom James was writing, could have faith in the Law or in the Temple or in what their Rabbi taught, but such faith would not save them.

We can have faith in our church tradition, in the teaching of liberal scholars, or in a god of our imagination, but such faith will not save us. We are saved by grace through faith in the Lord Jesus Christ, not *by* works, so that no-one can boast. However, we are saved *for* good works, and the good works are the evidence of that true faith. If we do not produce the good works, if we live immoral lives, then people have the right to question whether we are Christians and whether we have true faith. Let us live lives which will never give rise to such criticism.

"If I am saved by grace through faith and not by works, that means I can do what I like," said the student! "Yes!" said the teacher, "and you tell me what you like doing, and I will tell you if your faith is real."

21 Greeks are Jews
True or false?

Some have suggested that the word *Hellenes*, translated "Greek" in the New Testament, does **not** describe Gentiles, but is referring to Hellenised Israelites. They state that it does **not** refer to Gentiles who lived in the eastern half of the Roman Empire, spoke Greek, and who followed Hellenistic philosophy and teaching, customs, and behaviour.

Now it is true that practically all Jews, both those living in the land of Israel and those scattered throughout the Roman Empire and beyond, spoke Greek. After all, the *Septuagint* (LXX), a translation of the Old Testament from Hebrew into Greek, had been made well over 100 years before Christ was born, and this was because, by then, the majority of Jews spoke Greek, and only a few knew Hebrew.

It is also true that some of the Jews in the eastern half of the Roman Empire had become quite lax in their observance of the Law of Moses. For example, some no longer circumcised their children, and some who had been circumcised tried to reverse it (Acts 16:1-3). Few attended the feasts at the temple in Jerusalem: consider Acts 2 and the list of places from where the Jews came, and note the absence of Jews from places in the eastern half of the Roman Empire such as Antioch in Pisidia, Iconium, Lystra, Derbe, and so on. However, the issue is not whether or not certain Jews had become Hellenised; some had. The issue is: does the New Testament refer to them as "Greeks"?

Greeks in the Gospels

We read in John 12:20 that in Jerusalem "there were some Greeks among those who went up to worship at the Feast". This, say some, shows that the term "Greeks" refers to Jews because Gentiles did not go up to Jerusalem to worship at the temple. However, this is simply incorrect. Any diagram of the Jerusalem Temple shows that the outer courts were called the "Court of the Gentiles" which was separated from the inner courts by a wall (see diagram on the next page). Posted on the entrances in this wall to the inner courts was a notice, stating that no uncircumcised person could enter, and if he did so, it was upon the pain of death.

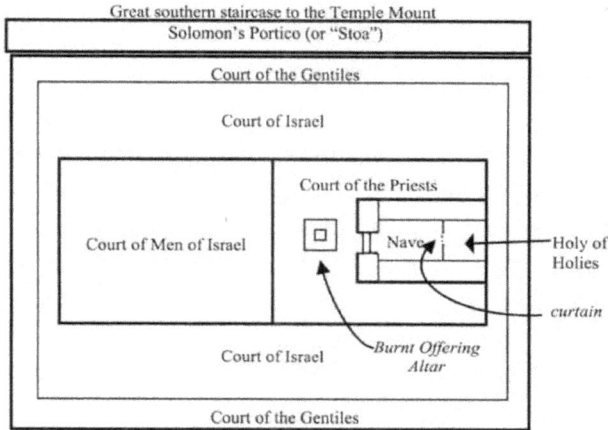

In the Gospels we read also (in Matthew 15:22-28) that a Canaanite woman from that vicinity came to him, crying out, "Lord, Son of David, have mercy on me! My daughter is suffering terribly from demon-possession." However, Jesus did not answer a word. So his disciples came to him and urged him, "Send her away, for she keeps crying out after us." Christ answered them with, "I was sent only to the lost sheep of Israel." So clearly this woman was not a Jew.

Nevertheless, the woman came and knelt before him. "Lord, help me!" she said. He replied, "It is not right to take the children's bread and toss it to their dogs." "Yes, Lord," she said, "but even the dogs eat the crumbs that fall from their masters' table." 'Dogs' was a term Jews used of Gentiles and, in using this description of her, Christ acknowledged that she was a Gentile; and in using the term of herself she admitted she was a Gentile.

However, in the parallel passage in Mark 7:26-28 we read that the woman was a 'Greek', born in Syrian Phoenicia. She begged Jesus to drive the demon out of her daughter. "First let the children eat all they want," he told her, "for it is not right to take the children's bread and toss it to their dogs." "Yes, Lord," she replied, "but even the dogs under the table eat the children's crumbs." So here a 'Greek' was not one of the lost sheep of the house of Israel. She was, in fact, a Syro-Phoenician 'dog', a Gentile.

Greeks in Acts

In Acts 11:19-20, we read that those who had been scattered by the persecution in connection with Stephen travelled as far as Phoenicia, Cyprus and Antioch, telling the message only to Jews. Some of them, however, men from Cyprus and Cyrene, went to *Antioch* and began to speak to "Greeks" also, telling them the good news about the Lord Jesus. Now were these Hellenised Jews living in Antioch, or were they Gentiles? Antioch was in Syria, north of Galilee. It was not in Greece, or Macedonia or Asia.

As we read through Acts we find that these 'Greeks' in Antioch were being pressurised into being circumcised (Acts 15:1). However, in Acts 15:3 these 'Greeks' are called 'Gentiles'. Then, at the Jerusalem Council which debated this issue, the apostles and elders met and made the decision that these people did not need to be circumcised, and they sent their decision in a letter. This letter was from "The apostles and elders" and was addressed "To the *Gentile* believers in Antioch, Syria and Cilicia." Thus those called 'Greeks' in Acts 11:20 are called 'Gentiles' in both Acts 15:3 and 15:23.

In Acts 16:1-3 we read about Paul circumcising Timothy.

> He came to Derbe and then to Lystra, where a disciple named Timothy lived, whose mother was a Jewess and a believer, but whose father was a Greek. The brothers at Lystra and Iconium spoke well of him. Paul wanted to take him along on the journey, so he circumcised him because of the Jews who lived in that area, for they all knew that his father was a Greek.

It is clear that Timothy's mother had been rather lax. She had married a Greek (Gentile) and did not have her son circumcised. However, she is called a 'Jewess', not a 'Greek woman', as some Gentile women were called (Acts 17:12). She may well have been a Hellenised Israelite but she was still a Jewess.

At that time there were many Jews scattered throughout the Roman Empire and beyond, and they did influence the societies in which they lived and some of the Gentiles attended the synagogues. Some, in accordance with the Law of Moses, became circumcised and kept the Sabbath, and these were known as Proselytes and were considered Jews (Isaiah 56:6-7). They could enter the body of the synagogue and the inner courts of the Jerusalem temple. Others, who for one reason or another did not undertake the rite of circumcision, were called God-fearers: e.g. Cornelius in Acts 10:1-2. They did not enter the main body of the synagogue and could attend only the outer courts of the temple.

In many of the synagogues Paul visited there were Jews and Proselytes, and also God-fearers, and so we read such things as: "Some of the Jews were persuaded and joined Paul and Silas, as did a large number of God-fearing Greeks and not a few prominent women ... Many of the Jews believed, as did also a number of prominent Greek women and many Greek men" (Acts 17:4,12). Here the God-fearing Greeks are distinguished from the Jews; see also Acts 17:17; 18:4; 19:10,17

We also read in Acts 21:27-29 that some Jews from the province of Asia saw Paul at the temple. They stirred up the whole crowd and seized him, shouting, "Men of Israel, help us! This is the man who teaches all men everywhere against our people and our law and this place. And besides, he has brought Greeks into the temple area and defiled this holy place." (They had previously seen Trophimus the Ephesian in the city with Paul and assumed that Paul had brought him into the temple area.)

There are two things to note here: first Trophimus from Ephesus is called a Greek, and second that their concern was that he had been taken into the inner courts of the temple, not the outer courts, the Court of the Gentiles.

Greeks in the Letters.

In Galatians 2:3 Paul wrote: "Yet not even Titus, who was with me, was compelled to be circumcised, even though he was a Greek." This indicates that Titus was a Gentile, for if he had been a Hellenised Israelite, as Timothy and his family were, Paul would have circumcised him as he had done Timothy (Acts 16:1-3).

In the letters we also have a number of similar passages which refer to Greeks. For example:

- 1 Corinthians 12:13: whether Jews or Greeks, slave or free.
- Galatians 3:28: There is neither Jew nor Greek, slave nor free, male nor female.
- Colossians 3:11: Here there is no Greek or Jew, circumcised or uncircumcised, barbarian, Scythian, slave or free.

In these passages pairs of words are used to describe people, and these words are mutually exclusive, and so by using these pairs all people were covered.

- A person was either slave or not a slave (i.e. free) and so everyone is covered.
- A person was either circumcised or not-circumcised, there was no intermediate state; thus everyone is included.
- A person was either a Jew or not a Jew (i.e. a Greek, a Gentile), and so everyone was considered.

To make Greek mean Hellenised Jew would imply that in the pair of words "Jew or Greek" the vast majority of the population (the Gentile population) was excluded. This is not the case in the other pairs "male or female" and "slave or free".

- A person is either a male or a female.
- Either a person is a slave, or is free.
- Either a person is a Jew, or a Greek: i.e. he is not a Jew but a Gentile.

Greeks

Two words are used with reference to 'Greeks' in the New Testament: *Hellenes* and *Hellenistai*. The term *Hellenes* refers to the inhabitants of Greece or their descendants (cf. Acts 16:1; Romans 1:14); but it is also used as a virtual equivalent of 'Gentile', to describe those who are not of Jewish origin (c.f. Romans 10:12; Galatians 3:28).

The term *Hellenistai* is a crux. It is confined to Acts 6:1; 9:29 (where A reads *Hellenas*) and 11:20 (as a variant reading, though *Hellenas,* Aleph^c A D*1518, is probably to be preferred).

C F D Moule points out (*Expository Times* LXX, 1958-9, p 100) that the objection to the traditional interpretation of *Hellenistai* as 'Greek-speaking Jews' is that Paul, who spoke Greek, called himself *Hebraios* (Philippians 3:5), which in Acts 6:1 forms the contrast to *Hellenistai*. He therefore proposes 'Jews who spoke *only* Greek' as the meaning of *Hellenistai*, and 'Jews who, while able to speak Greek, knew a Semitic language *also*' as the meaning of *Hebraioi*.

(*New Bible Dictionary*, page 494, IVP, 1975)

Comment

Hellenas is likely to be the correct reading in Acts 11:20 rather than *Hellenistai*, for if the latter then these Greek speaking Jews of Acts 11:20 are later called 'Gentiles' in Acts 15:23, and there is no way that the *Hellenistai* of Acts 6:1 and 9:29 could be countenanced as Gentiles, for they lived and attended synagogues in Jerusalem.

22 Missionaries should take the gospel to the Jews first
True or false?

In Romans 1:16 Paul, writing to the Roman Christians of that time, stated, "I am not ashamed of the gospel, because it is the power of God for the salvation of everyone who believes: first for the Jew, then for the Gentile."

Because of that statement, some present-day Gentile Christians believe that their primary missionary efforts, whether in giving or witnessing (at home or abroad), should be directed to Jews and those Missionary organisations working exclusively amongst the Jews. However, a serious misconception would seem to lie in a failing to understand what the situation was when Paul wrote to the Romans, and the change there was in God's plan which came about within a few years of the writing of this epistle.

Jewish Dominance

Abraham is first mentioned in Genesis 11 and, although we see God working with others, his story occupies much of the rest of the book and, by the time we reach the end of Genesis, Abraham's descendants dominate what we read. They had been told that they would occupy first place in God's plan for this world; others would be blessed through them and they would be a kingdom of priests to the other nations.

> The LORD had said to Abram, "Go from your country, your
> people and your father's household to the land I will show you.
> I will make you into a great nation,
>   and I will bless you;
> I will make your name great,
>   and you will be a blessing.
> I will bless those who bless you,
>   and whoever curses you I will curse;

and all peoples on earth
    will be blessed through you." (Genesis 12:1-3)

"'Now if you obey me fully and keep my covenant, then out of all nations you will be my treasured possession. Although the whole earth is mine, you[J] will be for me a kingdom of priests and a holy nation.' These are the words you are to speak to the Israelites." (Exodus 19:5-6)

However, once we get into Exodus and beyond, we find that the rest of the Old Testament is almost exclusively Jewish. And it doesn't stop there – so are the Gospels! Our Lord Jesus Christ is recorded as having very few dealings with Gentiles, just on two or three occasions, and He told his disciples not to go to the Gentiles, but only to the people of Israel. He also stated that He, himself, was sent "only to the lost sheep of Israel" (Matthew 10:5-6; 15:24).

Christ fully supported the Mosaic Law: not the least stroke of a pen from the Law would be done away with until all was fulfilled, He said (Matthew 5:17-18).

And in Romans 15:8, Paul described our Saviour as "a minister of Israel" (*KJV*); "a servant of the Jews[20]" (*NIV*). He most certainly was the Saviour of the World, the Lamb of God who took away the sin of the world, but His ministry when on earth was almost exclusively Jewish.

The Acts of the Apostles

Following His resurrection the disciple's burning question to our Lord was "Will you at this time restore the kingdom to Israel?" (Acts 1:6). This would surely indicate that Israel was not set aside by God at the cross; and that the church of today could not have begun at Pentecost, for Pentecost was, after all, the fulfilment of one of the Jewish Feasts of

---

[20] 'Israel' (*KJV*) and 'Jew' (*NIV*) is 'circumcision' in the Greek; i.e. Christ was a minister / servant of the circumcision.

Leviticus 23, just as Passover was. The Gentile Church of this age of grace in which we live could not have started then.

Scripture shows clearly and unambiguously that Israel were not set aside at the Cross or at Pentecost. A good demonstration of this may be found in the frequency of certain words in the Acts of the Apostles. Consider, for example, the occurrences of such words as Abraham, Isaac, Jacob, Israel, Israelite, Hebrew(s), Jew(s) and Jewish, in the four quarters of the Acts of the Apostles. The table shows the number of occurrences.

From this we can note two things:

1) that Israel dominates the Acts of the Apostles, and
2) that they are just as much to the forefront in the second half of Acts as they are in the first half.

Acts chapters	Number of occurrences
1 - 7	35
8 - 14	29
15 - 21	39
22 - 28	31

By contrast the word "Gentile(s)" occurs just 6 times in the last quarter of Acts.

Furthermore, if we read the Scriptures diligently, we will find that during the Acts period all the missionary work was done by Jews; all the teaching was done by Jews; and all the leaders in the newly-formed local Christian communities were Jews. All of this was in accordance with the Old Testament teaching that others would be blessed through the Jews.

So the Jews did, during the time covered by the Acts of the Apostles, continue to occupy first place in God's purposes. His main purpose was for Israel to become a Kingdom of Priests to the other nations of the world; (see Exodus 19:5-6 quoted on the previous page).

It was only right and proper that they were given every opportunity (and the first opportunity) to believe in Jesus as the Christ (their Messiah), the Son of God and their Saviour. Thus the Gospel was to go to them first, which is precisely what Paul did on his missionary journeys.

Then Paul and Barnabas answered them boldly: 'We had to speak the word of God to you first. Since you reject it and do not consider yourselves worthy of eternal life, we now turn to the Gentiles. (Acts 13:46)

When they had passed through Amphipolis and Apollonia, they came to Thessalonica, where there was a Jewish synagogue. As his custom was, Paul went into the synagogue, and on three Sabbath days he reasoned with them from the Scriptures. (Acts 17:1-2)

He continued going to the Jewish synagogues first on all his missionary journeys, and even right at the end of Acts, when he got to Rome, he did not call to him the Christian leaders, but rather "the leaders of the Jews" (Acts 28:17).

The change

But things were soon to change. As was the case elsewhere, the Jewish leaders in Rome could not agree amongst themselves as to whether or not Jesus was the Messiah (Acts 28:24-25). The Jews in the land had, by and large, rejected Christ in person. Then, during the Acts period, the Jews outside the land rejected the preaching of Christ. Thus in Acts 28:25-27 we have the last pronouncement of Isaiah's judgmental prophecy that Israel.

> Go to this people and say, 'You will be ever hearing but never understanding; you will be ever seeing but never perceiving.'
> For this people's heart has become calloused; they hardly hear with their ears, and they have closed their eyes. Otherwise they might see with their eyes, hear with their ears, understand with their hearts and turn, and I would heal them." (Act 28:26-27)

Because of their hardened heart, the Jews were blind to the message and deaf to the word of the Apostles. God's salvation was to be sent to the Gentiles (Acts 28:28).

Following that momentous statement Paul wrote seven letters – Ephesians, Philippians, Colossians, 1 & 2 Timothy, Titus and Philemon. In these we read of a new situation. The Mosaic Law was abolished for the Jews.

> For he himself is our peace, who has made the two groups one and has destroyed the barrier, the dividing wall of hostility, by setting aside in his flesh the law with its commandments and regulations. His purpose was to create in himself one new man out of the two, thus making peace, and in one body to reconcile both of them to God through the cross, by which he put to death their hostility. (Ephesians 2:14-16)

> When you were dead in your sins and in the uncircumcision of your sinful nature, God made you alive with Christ. He forgave us all our sins, having cancelled the written code, with its regulations, that was against us and that stood opposed to us; he took it away, nailing it to the cross ... Therefore do not let anyone judge you by what you eat or drink, or with regard to a religious festival, a New Moon celebration or a Sabbath day. These are a shadow of the things that were to come; the reality, however, is found in Christ. (Colossians 2:13-17)

We also learn that from then on Jewish and Gentile Christians were equal; they were one.

> This mystery is that through the gospel the Gentiles are heirs together with Israel, members together of one body, and sharers together in the promise in Christ Jesus. (Ephesians 3:6)

In fact Ephesians 3:6 states that believers from all nations are equal-heirs, equal-members and equal-sharers in this new church, the Body of Christ. And that includes any Jewish Christians. They are no longer first and foremost. They no longer have the privileges and blessings they had during the Old Testament, the Gospels and Acts period. And no longer does the gospel have to go to them first.

23 Trouble and distress, glory and honour, will fall on the Jew first
True or false?

In Romans 2:9-10, Paul wrote, "There will be trouble and distress for every human being who does evil: first for the Jew, then for the Gentile; but glory, honour and peace for everyone who does good: first for the Jew, then for the Gentile." What does Paul mean here? And is that still true in this age of grace in which we live?

Paul wrote those words during the time covered by the Acts of the Apostles and he wrote them to *Christians*. He wrote to the Roman Christians telling them that:

> ... because of your stubbornness and your unrepentant heart, you are storing up wrath against yourself for the day of God's wrath, when his righteous judgment will be revealed. God "will give to each person according to what he has done." To those who by persistence in doing good seek glory, honour and immortality, he will give eternal life. But for those who are self-seeking and who reject the truth and follow evil, there will be wrath and anger. There will be trouble and distress for every human being who does evil: first for the Jew, then for the Gentile; but glory, honour and peace for everyone who does good: first for the Jew, then for the Gentile. (Romans 2:5-10)

Here we read that the Roman Christians, because of their stubborn and unrepentant hearts, were storing up wrath and judgment. There would be trouble and distress for all who were self-seeking and who followed evil ways, but this judgment would fall upon the Jews first. However, for those Christians who were persistent in doing good, there would be glory and honour, but again, the Jews would receive such blessings first.

The Acts of the Apostles

If we read the Acts of the Apostles carefully, paying attention to what is said and *to whom* it is said (or about), we will notice that there are several differences between what is said of Jews and what is said of Gentiles. And again, we will notice differences between what is said of those Jews who had believed in Jesus and those who did not. That is, we need to distinguish between Christian Jews and non-Christian Jews, just as we would distinguish between Christian Gentiles and non-Christian Gentiles.

Now the remarkable thing about this passage in Romans is that it is *not* talking about non-Christians, but about Christians: trouble and distress were to fall upon Christians! Christian Jews first, and then Christian Gentiles. However, there were to be blessings upon other Christians and again, the Christian Jew would receive them first, before the Christian Gentile.

The first thing we need to do is to remove from our minds that such judgments have anything to do with eternity. Whether Jew or Gentile, the Christians of that time rejoiced in the truth that as far as eternity was concerned, there was no condemnation for those who are in Christ Jesus (Romans 8:1); they knew they had eternal life in Christ. But there was something going on during the Acts period which was special and peculiar to that time, and it should not be taken into this age of grace in which we live.

Miraculous Signs

When our Lord was on earth He did many miraculous signs in accordance with Isaiah 35:3-6:

> Strengthen the feeble hands,
>   steady the knees that give way;
> say to those with fearful hearts,
>   'Be strong, do not fear;
> your God will come,

he will come with vengeance;
with divine retribution
he will come to save you.'
Then will the eyes of the blind be opened
and the ears of the deaf unstopped.
Then will the lame leap like a deer,
and the mute tongue shout for joy.

And, at the end of his Gospel, John stated that these signified that He was the Christ (Messiah), the Son of God (John 20:30-31).

> Jesus performed many other miraculous signs in the presence of his disciples, which are not recorded in this book. But these are written that you may believe that Jesus is the Messiah, the Son of God, and that by believing you may have life in his name. (John 20:30-31)

These miracles are termed by some theologians as 'evidential' miracles as their purpose was to provide evidence to the Jews that Jesus was their Messiah. These miraculous signs continued into the Acts of the Apostles, and so we see the Apostles healing 'in the name of Jesus'. But something was added during Acts. As well as the miraculous sign of healing, there was also the miraculous sign of judgment.

Israel had been told in Deuteronomy 28 that if they obeyed they would have blessings, but if they did not there would be judgments, and they were told that these were to be signs to them and their descendants (see Deuteronomy 28:1-2,15,45-46). Israel were not cast aside by God at the Cross or at Pentecost (as any careful reading of Acts will show), and it seems that this situation of blessings and judgments continued for the next 30 or so years, until the end of the Acts period.

Judgments

We see a Jew and Jewess, Ananias and Sapphira, judged for lying in Acts 5. They were both Christians but they were struck dead, and a similar fate awaited the King of the Jews, Herod Agrippa, who did not give God the glory (Acts 12:19-23), an event which is vividly described by Josephus in *Antiquities of the Jews*, (19,8,2) – both quoted in full in the Appendix at the end of the chapter. Then the Jewish sorcerer Elymas was struck blind for opposing Paul (Acts 13:6-12).

In the letter to James, written during the Acts period and addressed to Christians from "The twelve tribes scattered among the nations" (James 1:1), we read of those who, through sinning, had fallen ill. The Jewishness of this is self-evident as it talks about the anointing with oil (James 5:14-16).

And Paul deals with a similar problem in the Jewish section of 1 Corinthians, which commences at 1 Corinthians 10:1 and runs for two chapters, before Paul addresses the Gentile Christians in 1 Corinthians 12:1-2. In the Jewish section we read of Christians who were not only ill, but who had also died as a result of judgment, for drunkenness and gluttony at their love feasts when they were supposedly remembering the Lord's death and celebrating the Lord's Supper.

> Everyone ought to examine themselves before they eat of the bread and drink from the cup. For those who eat and drink without discerning the body of Christ eat and drink judgment on themselves. That is why many among you are weak and ill, and a number of you have fallen asleep. (1 Corinthians 11:28-30).

And we read in John, who also wrote to Jewish Christians, about the "sin that leads to death". He implied that there was little point in praying for Christians who had committed such a sin.

> If you see any brother or sister commit a sin that does not lead to death, you should pray and God will give them life. I refer to those whose sin does not lead to death. There is a sin that leads to death. I am not saying that you should pray about that. All wrongdoing is sin, and there is sin that does not lead to death. (1 John 5:16-17)

Again, please note: this does not mean to say that such Christian Jews lost their salvation or eternal life: there is no eternal condemnation for those who are in Christ. However, they were, during the time covered by the Acts of the Apostle, still subject to the Law of Moses in general and Deuteronomy 28 in particular[21]. And so we see that the words of Paul in Romans 2:9-10 are backed up by other Scripture.

That was the situation during the time covered by the Acts of the Apostles. This was what happened at that time, but it does not happen today. Acts is descriptive of what was happening then; it is not prescriptive of what should happen today.

So we see that trouble and distress did fall upon Jewish Christians during the Acts period, and it did fall upon them first. In fact there is no passage which tells us that any judgment fell specifically upon a Gentile Christian, although they may have been included in the group Paul mentions in 1 Corinthians 11:28-30.

Blessings

As we read through the Acts of the Apostles we see clearly the blessing of healing falling upon the Jews first – there being no Gentiles around for the first part of the book. However, we do see Gentiles being healed later in Lystra (Acts 14:8-18) and on Malta (Acts 28:7-9).

The Jews also, at that time, had the honour of being the missionaries, the teachers and the leaders, and there are no references in Acts, or any of the letters written during that time, that Gentiles held any such positions. That came later, after Acts.

The Jews also had the gospel preached to them first, in accordance with Romans 1:16, and during Acts we see that the first place Paul visited in any city on his journeys was the Jewish synagogue. Thus the Jews were the first to receive that peace of God which passes understanding.

---

[21] For more on this important chapter please see *Deuteronomy 28: A Key to Understanding* by Michael Penny.

The Age of Grace

We live in the "administration of God's grace" (Ephesians 3:2), which commenced at the end of Acts, following the final pronouncement of Isaiah's judgmental prophecy in Acts 28:25-27. There God revealed that His salvation was to be sent to the Gentiles (Acts 28:28). There was certainly grace in evidence before then, not only in the Acts and the Gospels, but also in the Old Testament. After all "Abraham believed God and it was counted to him as righteousness" (Genesis 15:6). Thus Abraham was not saved by works, but by grace.

However, throughout that period grace did not reign; there were blessings and there were judgements, as we have seen. But in an "administration of grace" grace reigns and God either acts graciously or not at all. There is no place for judgments, and there are no direct judgments from God today.

Also, no group of Christians has privileges or priorities over any other group, and so we read in Ephesians 3:6 that "The Gentiles are heirs together with Israel, members together of one body, and sharers together in the promise in Christ Jesus". All Christians, no matter what their race, are equal heirs, equal members and equal sharers in the Body of Christ. No group has the blessings first, for after all, we *all* are blessed in the heavenly realms with *every* spiritual blessing (Ephesians 1:3). And no group has the judgement first – in fact there are no judgments!

****

Appendix: The Death of Herod Agrippa ...

... In the Bible (Acts 12:19-23)

Then Herod went from Judea to Caesarea and stayed there. He had been quarrelling with the people of Tyre and Sidon; they now joined together and sought an audience with him. After securing the support of Blastus, a trusted personal servant of the king, they asked for peace, because they depended on the king's country for their food supply.

On the appointed day Herod, wearing his royal robes, sat on his throne and delivered a public address to the people. They shouted, 'This is the voice of a god, not of a man.' Immediately, because Herod did not give praise to God, an angel of the Lord struck him down, and he was eaten by worms and died.

... In Josephus (The Antiquities of the Jews 19,8,2)

Now when Agrippa had reigned three years over all Judea, he came to the city Caesarea, which was formerly called Strato's Tower; and there he exhibited shows in honour of Caesar, upon his being informed that there was a certain festival celebrated to make vows for his safety. At which festival a great multitude was gotten together of the principal persons, and such as were of dignity through his province.

On the second day of which shows he put on a garment made wholly of silver, and of a contexture truly wonderful, and came into the theatre early in the morning; at which time the silver of his garment being illuminated by the fresh reflection of the sun's rays upon it, shone out after a surprising manner, and was so resplendent as to spread a horror over those that looked intently upon him; and presently his flatterers cried out, one from one place, and another from another, (though not for his good,) that he was a god; and they added, "Be thou merciful to us; for although we have hitherto reverenced thee only as a man, yet shall we henceforth own thee as superior to mortal nature."

Upon this the king did neither rebuke them, nor reject their impious flattery. But as he presently afterward looked up, he saw an owl sitting on a certain rope over his head, and immediately understood that this bird was the messenger of ill tidings, as it had once been the messenger of good tidings to him; and fell into the deepest sorrow.

A severe pain also arose in his belly, and began in a most violent manner. He therefore looked upon his friends, and said, "I, whom you call a god, am commanded presently to depart this life; while Providence thus reproves the lying words you just now said to me; and I, who was by you called immortal, am immediately to be hurried away by death. But I am bound to accept of what Providence allots, as it pleases God; for we have by no means lived ill, but in a splendid and happy manner."

When he said this, his pain was become violent. Accordingly he was carried into the palace, and the rumour went abroad everywhere, that he would certainly die in a little time. But the multitude presently sat in sackcloth, with their wives and children, after the law of their country, and besought God for the king's recovery. All places were also full of mourning and lamentation.

 Now the king rested in a high chamber, and as he saw them below lying prostrate on the ground, he could not himself forbear weeping. And when he had been quite worn out by the pain in his belly for five days, he departed this life, being in the fifty-fourth year of his age, and in the seventh year of his reign; for he reigned four years under Caius Caesar, three of them were over Philip's tetrarchy only, and on the fourth he had that of Herod added to it; and he reigned, besides those, three years under the reign of Claudius Caesar; in which time he reigned over the aforementioned countries, and also had Judea added to them, as well as Samaria and Caesarea. The revenues that he received out of them were very great, no less than twelve millions of drachma. Yet did he borrow great sums from others; for he was so very liberal that his expenses exceeded his incomes, and his generosity was boundless.

24 There is an advantage is in being a Jew
True or false?

Fairly near the beginning of Romans Paul posed the question, "What advantage, then, is there in being a Jew, or what value is there in circumcision?" and answered it with a very emphatic "Much in every way!" (Romans 3:1-2). But is that true today? Is there an advantage in being a Jew today? There may have been in the Christian society of the time when Paul wrote (and Romans was written during the period covered by the Acts of the Apostles), but is there today, in this age of grace in which we live?

In the second half of verse 2 Paul gives the primary reason why there was an advantage in being a Jew. He states "First of all, they have been entrusted with the very words of God." In other words, the Jews of that period had a great advantage over the Gentiles of that time quite simply because they had the Scriptures and knew what they taught.

The People of the Acts Period

During New Testament times there were three quite different groups of people that we read about. First there were the Jews and Proselytes. These are one group. Jews, clearly, were descendants of Abraham through Isaac and Jacob. The Proselytes were Gentiles who had converted to Judaism (see Acts 1:11). These had to be circumcised, observe the Sabbath, and be diligent with the rest of the Law of Moses (e.g. Isaiah 56:6-7); they were then counted as Jews.

> "And foreigners who bind themselves to the LORD
>   to minister to him,
> to love the name of the LORD,
>   and to be his servants,
> all who keep the Sabbath without desecrating it
>   and who hold fast to my covenant [of circumcision] –
> these I will bring to my holy mountain

and give them joy in my house of prayer.
Their burnt offerings and sacrifices
   will be accepted on my altar;
for my house will be called
   a house of prayer for all nations." (Isaiah 56:6-7)

The Ethiopian Eunuch of Acts 8:26-38 must have been such a person, for only someone who had been circumcised could worship in the inner courts of the temple in Jerusalem, although uncircumcised people could visit the outer courts.

The God-fearers

The next group are those who are termed God-fearers. A number of the pagan Gentiles had become disillusioned with the idolatrous and immoral worship in the pagan temples. If you wanted to get drunk, you worshipped Bacchus! If you wanted sex, the temple of Zeus in Corinth had 1,000 priestesses, but we would call them prostitutes.

Thus some pagans were attracted to the Jewish religion by its simplicity, its morality, its sincerity; so much so that a number of the synagogues of that time had sections for Gentiles, either at the back or in a balcony.

During the years leading up to the Acts period, Judaism, for probably the only time in its history, embarked on proselytising with somewhat evangelical zeal. The Jews actively sought to encourage pagans to attend their synagogues, and then encouraged the God-fearing pagans to become circumcised, to keep the Sabbath and to become Proselytes: i.e. in effect to become Jews.

Two such people were the centurion in Capernaum, who built a synagogue (Luke 7:1-5), and Cornelius, also a centurion and described as God-fearing (Acts 10:2). And when Paul visited the synagogues on his journeys there were often God-fearing Gentiles present (see Acts 13:26,50; 17:4,17).

Pagans

The third and final group of people can be termed pagans. They would have been idolaters and some of them were converted in the market place and other public places where Paul and others preached. They came to Christianity direct from the pagan temples and they would not have had the moral background of the Jews, the Proselytes and the God-fearing Gentiles. This may explain why they come up with such wrong notions as "Shall we go on sinning that grace may abound?" (Romans 6:1) and why they fell back into sexual immorality (1 Corinthians 5:11).

The Word of God

A reading of the Acts and the letters written during that time will reveal that all the missionaries were Jews (or Proselytes), all the teaching was done by Jews (or Proselytes), and as far as we can see, all the leaders seem to be Jews (or Proselytes). There are a number of reasons for this and one of them is quite simply that they knew the word of God, the Scriptures.

Those Christians who were Jews (or Proselytes) had been taught the Scriptures from an early age and knew what they taught. Paul argued from the Law of Moses and the Prophets that Jesus was the Christ, the Son of God (Acts 28:23), and they could follow the argument, whether they agreed with it or not.

They had high morals, and knew what was right and wrong. What a tremendous advantage that was at that time. Even relatively new Proselytes would have to have undertaken a course of intense teaching in the Word of God before being circumcised.

As for the God-fearing Gentiles: I suspect some of them knew quite a lot but, for one reason or another, chose not to be circumcised and become Proselytes. One can well imagine why people like Cornelius or the Centurion in Capernaum did not do so. If they had become Proselytes the Romans would have moved them from Israel. However, it is more likely that most of the God-fearing Gentiles were not well versed in the

Scriptures and so were not in a position to be able to teach or evangelise. And as for those converted straight from paganism, clearly they were in need of much teaching and support.

The Administration of Grace

However, as we progress through the New Testament and leave the Acts of the Apostles, we enter the administration of grace (Ephesians 3:2). Now we see a change. The last letters Paul wrote all pertain to this age of grace in which we live, and were Ephesians, Philippians, Colossians, 1 & 2 Timothy, Titus, and Philemon. In these we initially read of gifts from the ascended Christ: gifts such apostles, prophets, evangelists and teachers. These were given for a short while until the Jewish and Gentile believers, who crossed from the Acts period into the administration of grace, became one in the faith (Ephesians 4:11-13). It is possible that some of the people whom Christ chose to fill these offices were Gentiles. By this time many years had passed and some of the Gentiles had been Christians for quite some time and would have become well acquainted with God's word.

However, a little later we read not of Christ-given gifts of apostles, prophets, evangelists and teachers, but of man-made appointments. In 1 Timothy 3 and Titus 1, written a few years after Ephesians, we read of people appointing other people as overseers, deacons and elders, and one suspects that many of these were Gentiles, for Paul mentions few Jews. For example he says of Aristarchus, Mark and Jesus-Justus, "These are the *only* Jews among my fellow-workers" (Colossians 4:10-11).

What advantage is there in being a Jew today?

So is there an advantage in being a Jew today? The answer must be "No!" When Paul wrote Romans they had the Scriptures, our Old Testament. However, today they do not have "the very words of God". They accept only part of the Word of God; the Old Testament, but not the New. Hence they are at a great disadvantage, which inhibits them from coming to know Jesus and in gaining an understanding of God's purpose for this age of grace. Of course, should a Jew come to believe in

Jesus as his Saviour he can bring insights, especially from the Old Testament, which many Gentiles fail to see. In reading some of the writings of these 'Messianic Jews', as they are often called, I have frequently found them to be excellent on the Old Testament, the Gospels and on Christology. However, I have often found a lack of appreciation and understanding of Paul's different ministries, especially his role as the Apostle to the Gentiles and what he taught in his later letters.

Of course, many Gentile Christians can leave the Bible unread, gathering dust on its shelf, and so they rapidly lose their advantage of having both Old and New Testaments.

25 The New Covenant belongs to Gentiles
True or false?

In quite a few Christian churches today (Gentile Christian churches) one hears much about the New Covenant and, on occasions, about other covenants. This is somewhat surprising, especially in the light of what Paul wrote in Romans 9. There we read:

> For I could wish that I myself were cursed and cut off from Christ for the sake of my people, those of my own race, the people of Israel. Theirs is the adoption to sonship; theirs the divine glory, *the covenants*, the receiving of the law, the temple worship and the promises. Theirs are the patriarchs, and from them is traced the human ancestry of the Messiah, who is God over all, for ever praised! Amen. (Romans 9:3-5)

Here Paul states that the covenants are Israel's. However, many Christians are taught that God finished with the people of Israel at the cross and that the church of today started at Pentecost, even though Pentecost is a Jewish Feast and what is recorded in Acts 2 is a fulfilment of Leviticus 23, just as Christ, Himself, fulfilled the Passover of that chapter.

Romans was written late in the Acts period, probably twenty years after the Cross, and Paul raised this issue there at the start of chapter 11. He asked "Did God then reject his people [Israel]?" and his answer is "By no means!" and any diligent reader of the New Testament will see this as obvious.

The Jew dominates the Acts of the Apostles. A number of letters were written specifically to them during that time: Hebrews, James, 1 & 2 Peter, 1,2,3 John, Jude, and Revelation. And Paul's earlier letters – Romans, 1 & 2 Corinthians, Galatians, 1 & 2 Thessalonians – were written to churches which were a mixture of Jewish and Gentile Christians. It is only at the end of Acts that we read that Israel have become blind and deaf due to a hardened heart, and that God's salvation was to be sent to the Gentile independently of the Jew (Acts 28:25-28).

What belongs to Israel?

However, during Acts some of Israel believed in Jesus and some did not; that nation was experiencing a "hardening in part" (Romans 11:25) and this grieved Paul. So much so that he wrote:

> I have great sorrow and unceasing anguish in my heart. For I could wish that I myself were cursed and cut off from Christ for the sake of my brothers, those of my own race, the people of Israel. (Romans 9:2-4)

He then went on to list all the privileges the people of Israel had at that time:

- Theirs is the adoption as sons;
- theirs the divine glory,
- the *covenants*,
- the receiving of the law,
- the temple worship and
- the promises.
- Theirs are the patriarchs, and
- from them is traced the human ancestry of Christ, who is God over all, forever praised! Amen. (Romans 9:4-5)

Thus Paul stated that the temple worship belonged to Israel, and no one would disagree with that. He also stated that theirs was the Mosaic Law, and no one could disagree with that. And the patriarchs were Jewish, and no one could deny that. And from them was the human ancestry of Christ, and that cannot be denied. And to them belonged the covenants, and yet many deny that! Why? Everything in the list belongs to Israel, including the covenants. All the covenants in Scripture, apart from the one made with Noah, were made with the people of Israel. What? Even the New Covenant?

The Old Covenant

The old, or first covenant, is set out in Exodus 19:3-9, where we read:

> Then Moses went up to God, and the Lord called to him from the mountain and said, "This is what you are to say to the house of Jacob and what you are to tell the people of Israel: 'You yourselves have seen what I did to Egypt, and how I carried you on eagles' wings and brought you to myself. Now if you obey me fully and keep my covenant, then out of all nations you will be my treasured possession. Although the whole earth is mine, you will be for me a kingdom of priests and a holy nation.' These are the words you are to speak to the Israelites."
>
> So Moses went back and summoned the elders of the people and set before them all the words the Lord had commanded him to speak. The people all responded together, "We will do everything the Lord has said." So Moses brought their answer back to the Lord.

This first covenant was a conditional one; both parties being active. If Israel did something, then God would do something. If Israel fully obeyed the Law of Moses, then they would be His treasured possession and God would make them a holy nation and a kingdom of priests to the other nations of the world. If they did not obey ...! But no covenant based on human obedience can last and within a short space of time Israel was worshipping the golden calf. And so it continued throughout the Old Testament. God was never going to get His treasured possession, His holy nation, His kingdom of priests, unless He did something different.

The New Covenant

The New Covenant is encapsulated in Jeremiah 31:31-34.

> **31** "The time is coming," declares the Lord, "when I will make a new covenant with the house of Israel and with the house of Judah.

32 It will not be like the covenant I made with their forefathers when I took them by the hand to lead them out of Egypt, because they broke my covenant, though I was a husband to them," declares the Lord.

33 "This is the covenant I will make with the house of Israel after that time," declares the Lord. "I will put my law in their minds and write it on their hearts. I will be their God, and they will be my people.

34 No longer will a man teach his neighbour, or a man his brother, saying, 'Know the Lord,' because they will all know me, from the least of them to the greatest," declares the Lord. "For I will forgive their wickedness and will remember their sins no more."

We need to note that this New Covenant is to be made with "the house of Israel and the House of Judah" (verse 31), not with Gentiles. The New Covenant is to be made with *the same people* who broke the first covenant (verse 32), not with Gentiles who had no part in the first covenant and so have no part in the second covenant.

Part of this New Covenant states that God is going to write the Law, the Mosaic Law, on the hearts of people (verse 33): that is upon the hearts of the people of Judah and Israel, not upon the hearts of Gentiles, who have never been part of the Mosaic Law, the Old Covenant.

And when this New Covenant eventually comes "they will all know" the Lord, "from the least of them to the greatest" (verse 34). Well, it must be pretty obvious that the New Covenant has never come in.

The New Covenant is certainly not in the Gentile world of today where, in many countries, less than 10% of the population know the Lord. And neither has it come in for the people of Israel and Judah; even less of the Jewish population today are Christians.

Throughout the Old Testament Israel continually failed to obey God[22]. During the Gospel period they rejected Jesus Christ and put Him on the cross. And during the Acts period they rejected the ministry of the Apostles, and had them stoned, imprisoned, and beaten. No, there has never been a time when the New Covenant can be said to have been in operation and its promises fulfilled.

This is my blood of the New Covenant (Luke 22:20)

For some the words of our Lord Jesus Christ in Luke 22:20 herald the bringing in of the New Covenant, but this cannot be so. It is certainly true that the New Covenant could not have come in *before* our Lord had made His sacrifice for sin. Part of the New Covenant promises that God is going to forgive Israel and Judah their wickedness and remember their sin no more, but this first required Christ's sacrifice for their sins.

The Apostles, during the Acts period, were called "ministers of the New Covenant" (2 Corinthians 3:6). They preached that it was possible for the New Covenant to come in: the people of Israel first had to accept Jesus as their Christ (Messiah), and then Christ would return (Acts 3:19-21), whereupon the kingdom upon the earth would be set up and the New Covenant would come into operation[23].

During the Acts Period the Jews (both Christians and non-Christian) still observed the Law of Moses (the old covenant) and we read in Hebrews 8:13 that the old covenant was obsolete and aging and was "soon to disappear". This verse shows us clearly that the New Covenant had not yet come in; the Old Covenant was still operating.

And the writer of Hebrews is still using the future tense to describe the time period when the New Covenant would come in. There we read:

---

[22] Read more about Israel's failures and its consequences in *Deuteronomy 28: A Key to Understanding* by Michael Penny.

[23] For more on this see Michael Penny's *The New Covenant. Who is it with? When is it for?*

The time is coming, declares the Lord, when I *will* make a new covenant with the house of Israel and the house of Judah. (Hebrews 8:8)

Thus the New Covenant was still future in New Testament times, when Hebrews was written, and the promises pertaining to the New Covenant have never yet been fulfilled.

However, again in Hebrews, we need to note that the Bible continues to state that this New Covenant is with the House of Israel and the House of Judah (Hebrews 8:8). It was not made with Gentiles and it is not with the church of this age of grace, the Body of Christ.

So what happened?

Clearly this New Covenant did not come in either at the Cross or during the Acts period. In fact it will not be ratified until Christ returns, when He gathers His elect from the four corners of the earth and all Israel will be saved (Matthew 24:31; Romans 11:26). So what happened to the Old Covenant?

Thirty years of opposing the miraculous signs and the preaching of the Apostles gave Israel a hardened heart, rendering them blind to the signs and deaf to the ministry. Thus God's salvation was sent to the Gentiles (Acts 28:25-28). This brought in the Age of Grace in which we live and we read in the next verses that Paul was under house arrest for two years. Two of the letters he wrote during that time were Ephesians and Colossians, and both of these tell us that the Old Covenant with its accompanying Mosaic Law was abolished – Ephesians 2:14-16; Colossians 2:13-17.

> For he himself is our peace, who has made the two groups one and has destroyed the barrier, the dividing wall of hostility, by setting aside in his flesh the law with its commandments and regulations. His purpose was to create in himself one new man out of the two, thus making peace, and in one body to reconcile

both of them to God through the cross, by which he put to death their hostility. (Ephesians 2:14-16)

> When you were dead in your sins and in the uncircumcision of your sinful nature, God made you alive with Christ. He forgave us all our sins, having cancelled the written code, with its regulations, that was against us and that stood opposed to us; he took it away, nailing it to the cross … Therefore do not let anyone judge you by what you eat or drink, or with regard to a religious festival, a New Moon celebration or a Sabbath day. These are a shadow of the things that were to come; the reality, however, is found in Christ. (Colossians 2:13-17)

Thus the Old Covenant was obsolete and aging during Acts and was soon to disappear, states Hebrews 8:13, written towards the end of the Acts Period. However, at the end of Acts it did disappear, but it was not replaced by the New Covenant, which will now not come in until Christ returns. The Old Covenant was replaced by the administration of grace (Ephesians 3:2).

Grace and Grace

However, both the New Covenant and the administration of grace are based on *grace*. In the New Covenant God is to forgive Israel their wickedness and remember their sins no more. In this administration of grace God has forgiven us "all our sins" (Colossians 2:13) and He certainly doesn't remember them for He sees us as being "holy in his sight – without blemish and free from accusation" (Colossians 1:22).

Thus although there are similarities between the New Covenant and the administration of grace, there are distinct differences. We do not live in a time when "No longer will a man teach his neighbour, or a man his brother, saying, 'Know the Lord,' because they will all know me, from the least of them to the greatest!" We still need to do the work of an evangelist (2 Timothy 4:5).

26 Gentiles are saved to make Israel envious
True or false?

One of the common misconceptions in Christendom today is to say that the Jew was set aside by God either at the Cross or on the Day of Pentecost. A diligent reading of the Acts of the Apostles rapidly shows this not to be the case, with over 130 references to the Jews or Hebrews in its 28 chapters, many more than to Gentiles.

In fact Gentiles do not appear on the scene until we come to the God-fearing Cornelius in Acts 10. These God-fearing Gentiles attended the synagogue but the Jews would still not enter their homes, hence Peter's dilemma. However, this was not against the Mosaic Law (*nomos*) but against the Jewish customs (*themis*) of their time, often originating from the Pharisaic additions to the Law of Moses – see Acts 10:28.

Peter's action caused consternation amongst the apostles and believers, and he was called to give an account of himself (Acts 11:1-18). However, we read nothing further of Peter, or any others from Jerusalem or Judea, visiting Gentiles until some Jewish Christians from Cyprus and Cyrene went to Antioch in Syria and began to speak to Greeks there (Acts 11:19-20). Yet again, this seems to have been an isolated incident and again it caused concern amongst the Jewish Christian leadership (compare Acts 11:1-3 and 11:22). It isn't until after Paul and Barnabas visit Jerusalem (mentioned in Acts 11:29-30 with more details given in Galatians 2:1-10) and they meet with Peter, James and John that things change. There they made an agreement that Paul and Barnabas would go to the Gentiles, while Peter, James and John would go to the Jews (Galatians 2:9).

However, we must be careful not to misunderstand this. This is not a racial division, but a geographical one, as Acts makes clear. Peter, James and John stayed in Jerusalem and Judea and worked with the Jews there, both those from the locality and those of the dispersion visiting the city. Paul and Barnabas travelled to the different nations (the Greek word *ethnos* can be translated 'nations' or 'Gentiles'). I suggest we should take a geographical interpretation of this agreement because, when Paul and Barnabas were on their travels, they always went first to the synagogues and preached to the Jews there. However, if the response was poor or mixed, then they turned to the Gentiles and preached to them. Why did they do that? And what was the effect?

The Jew first

God's desire was for Israel to become a Kingdom of Priests and take the message of their Messiah (Christ) to the ends of the earth (Exodus 19:5-6). However, they had rejected their Messiah, and crucified Him. On the Cross He prayed, "Father, forgive them, for they do not know what they are doing" (Luke 23:34). That prayer was answered and Israel were given a second chance, and Acts opens with the disciples asking Christ, "Lord, are you at this time going to restore the kingdom to Israel?" (Acts 1:6). To this Christ replied that it was not for them to know and from Peter's speech to the Jews in Acts 3:12-26, it seems it all depended upon whether Israel repented or not

> *Repent,* then, and turn to God, so that your sins may be wiped out, that times of refreshing may come from the Lord, and that he may *send the Christ*, who has been appointed for you—even Jesus. He must remain in heaven until the time comes for God to restore everything, as he promised long ago through his holy prophets. (Acts 3:19-21).

If they repented and turned to God not only would their sins be wiped out, but times of refreshing would come from the Lord, Christ would be sent back and all things would be restored, including the kingdom to Israel.

So what did happen? As we read through Acts, initially we see a great response from the ordinary Jews with thousands being saved (Acts 2:41; 4:4). However, soon there was strong opposition from the leadership (chapter 4); Stephen was stoned (chapter 7), and great persecution broke out (chapter 8). And this seems to be the pattern throughout Acts, with some Jews believing but many rejecting, especially the leaders. Only one Jewish ruler is mention as having believed in Christ: Crispus, the synagogue ruler in Corinth (Acts 18:8).

If that was the situation, it is perhaps not surprising that God should direct people like Paul not only to go to the Jews, but also to go to the Gentiles (Acts 9:15). However, for many Christians today, the reason God did this is quite surprising! Paul himself tells us why he went to the Gentiles at that time. In Romans 11:11-14 he asks and then answers the question:

> Again I ask: Did they [Israel] stumble so as to fall beyond recovery? Not at all! Rather, because of their transgression, salvation has come to the Gentiles *to make Israel envious*. But if their transgression means riches for the world, and their loss means riches for the Gentiles, how much greater riches will their fullness bring!
>
> I am talking to you Gentiles. Inasmuch as I am the apostle to the Gentiles, I make much of my ministry in the hope that I may somehow *arouse my own people to envy* and save some of them.

Romans was written quite late in the Acts period and Paul describes the rejection of Christ by some of the Jews, and especially the leadership, as a stumble, but one from which it was to recover. Later he was to describe the condition as "a hardening in part" (Romans 11:25).

He also wrote that "salvation has come to the Gentiles *to make Israel envious*", and he repeats this later by saying that he wanted somehow to "*arouse my own people to envy* and save some of them". The first thing we need to note is that this is **not** the reason why Gentiles are saved today in this age of grace in which we live. No Jew was envious when I was saved and none of the Jews I have met throughout my Christian life have ever appeared envious of the fact that I am a Christian. We must leave this statement in its historical situation.

The Acts Period

We have a detailed example of this envy in Acts 13:13-48. On their first journey Paul and Barnabas visited Galatia and went to Antioch in Pisidia. On the Sabbath they went to the synagogue and were invited to speak. Paul addressed the Jews and the God-fearing Gentiles who worshipped there. The result was very positive. They were invited back the next Sabbath day, and many of the Jews and Proselytes (Gentiles who had earlier converted to Judaism) followed Paul and Barnabas and discussed with them what had been said (verses 42-43).

This must have been a great subject of conversation in Antioch during the following week because on the next Sabbath almost the whole city gathered to hear the word of the Lord (v 44). However, when those Jews who did not believe that Jesus was the Christ saw the crowds, they were filled with envy.

Now envy is a strange thing. It can motivate people to emulate the people they envy and this, according to Romans 11:11-14, was the desired goal. Paul stated that Gentile salvation was "to arouse my own people [Israel] to envy and *save* some of them". That's what the Lord wanted. He wanted to lift Israel from their stumble. He wanted to soften their partially hardened heart. Would the salvation of the Gentiles achieve this?

As said above, envy is a strange thing because it can also cause people to become bitter towards the ones they envy, and this is what happened in Antioch. When the Jews who did not believe saw the crowds, they were filled with envy and ... they were filled with jealousy ... and talked abusively against what Paul was saying. Eventually they stirred up such persecution that they expelled Paul and Barnabas from that region (Acts 13:50).

And as we read through Acts we see this pattern repeated nearly everywhere that Paul went. At Iconium a great number of Jews and Gentiles believed, but the Jews who refused to believed stirred up trouble and there was a plot to stone Paul and Barnabas (Acts 14:1-5), and in Lystra Paul was actually stoned and left for dead (Acts 14:19-20).

The end of Acts

Clearly such a situation could not go on forever. When Paul eventually arrived in Rome he called the leaders of the Jews together and explained to them from the Law of Moses and the Prophets that Jesus was the Christ (Messiah), the Son of God. As usual some believed and some did not, but enough was enough (Acts 28:17-24).

Enough was indeed enough! By this time Israel had stumbled beyond recovery. Their heart had become so hardened that they did not hear what the apostles were saying, and they did not see the significance of the miraculous signs they were performing (Acts 28:25-27). This was the point at which Israel were set aside; *not* at the Cross. This was the time when the age of grace started and the church, the Body of Christ, commenced; *not* on the Day of Pentecost. This was when God's salvation was freely sent to the Gentiles (Acts 28:28), not to make Israel envious but "because of his great love for us, God, who is rich in mercy, made us alive with Christ, even when we were dead in transgressions – it is by grace you have been saved" (Ephesians 2:4-5).

No! I was not saved to make any Jew jealous, and neither is anyone else today.

27 Gentile Christians are grafted into the olive tree of Israel
True or false?

Romans 11:17-24

If some of the branches have been broken off, and you [Gentiles], though a wild olive shoot, have been grafted in among the others and now share in the nourishing sap from the olive root, do not boast over those branches. If you do, consider this: You do not support the root, but the root supports you. You will say then, "Branches were broken off so that I could be grafted in." Granted. But they were broken off because of unbelief, and you stand by faith. Do not be arrogant, but be afraid. For if God did not spare the natural branches, he will not spare you either.

Consider therefore the kindness and sternness of God: sternness to those who fell, but kindness to you, provided that you continue in his kindness. Otherwise, you also will be cut off. And if they do not persist in unbelief, they will be grafted in, for God is able to graft them in again. After all, if you were cut out of an olive tree that is wild by nature, and contrary to nature were grafted into a cultivated olive tree, how much more readily will these, the natural branches, be grafted into their own olive tree!

In Romans 11 Paul described how the Gentiles of that time (i.e. the Acts Period, for Romans was written during that time) were grafted into the olive tree of Israel. However, a number of Christians today believe that this is the position of the current Gentile church, the Body of Christ; but is this possible? Let us look at what was happening at the time Paul wrote, to see whether or not the words of Romans 11 can apply outside of that time.

The Acts Period

The people of Israel had rejected Christ in person and handed him over to be crucified. However, on the Cross the Saviour prayed, "Father, forgive them, for they do not know what they are doing" (Luke 23:34). That prayer for the people of Israel was clearly answered, as a straight reading of the Acts of the Apostles will show. The Jews dominate the Acts with there being well over 120 references to them in the 28 chapters of Acts.

God's plan for Israel was that they were to be a Kingdom of Priests to the Gentile nations, taking the message of Christ to the ends of the earth. The rejection and crucifixion of Christ was a setback, but Christ had to die and be the sin offering for both Israel and the rest of the world. Thus Acts opens with the question, "Lord, are you at this time going to restore the kingdom to Israel?" (Acts 1:6). However, the Lord would not answer the question, but the Holy Spirit, through Peter, stated that things would be restored if Israel repented (Acts 3:19-21). Initially thousands were saved, but there was great opposition from the leaders of Israel (Acts 4:1-22), culminating with a great persecution at the hands of Saul of Tarsus (Acts 8:1-3).

Following his conversion, Paul set about visiting the different countries of the eastern half of the Roman Empire, only to be met with opposition. He always visited the Jewish synagogue first and there some Jews believed and some did not, and those who did not stirred up great trouble for Paul; then he often turned to the Gentiles and preached to them, even in the market place. This infuriated the Jews who would not believe and often they hounded Paul out of town or imprisoned him or even stoned him.

This was the situation when Paul wrote Romans. But in Romans 11:1 Paul makes it clear that God had not, at the time of writing Romans, rejected His people Israel. He described the situation which existed during the Acts period as one in which Israel had stumbled, but not beyond recovery (Romans 11:11). He said that the nation of Israel had experienced a "hardening in part" (Romans 11:25).

In an attempt to provoke Israel to respond and accept Jesus as their Christ (Messiah), the message of salvation was being taken to the Gentiles and a number of them were saved. And Paul states that Gentile salvation at that time (i.e. during the Acts period) was "to make Israel envious" (Romans

11:11), in the hope that somehow the Jews would be aroused and saved (Romans 11:14).

The Olive Tree

In Romans 11:17-24 Paul gave an illustration of how this salvation of Gentiles might provoke Israel. Israel is likened to a cultivated olive tree; the Gentiles are a wild olive.

The cultivated olive tree of Israel was not bearing fruit, so what was to be done? In those days, when an olive tree grew old and the fruit became stony with little flesh, olive farmers were reluctant to cut the tree down. This was because any newly planted tree would not bear any fruit for decades: maybe sixty or seventy years. Thus in olive agriculture a technique had been developed by which an old tree could be invigorated into bearing good fruit for many more years.

Some of the natural branches were cut off and in their place branches from a wild olive were grafted in. The hope was that the life and vigour from the wild olive branches would stimulate the old tree into bearing fruit. Maybe it did not work with the first graft or two, and the process had to be repeated again in a few years' time. However, there was a limit to the number of wild olive branches that could be grafted in. Eventually the cultivated olive would really become a wild olive if too many wild branches were used.

This is exactly what was happening with Israel and the Gentiles during Acts (e.g. see Acts 13:44-46), and it went on nearly everywhere, not only in Jerusalem and Antioch in Syria but in practically every city Paul visited. It went on year after year; some of Israel believed, and some did not, and when Paul turned to the Gentiles, those Jews who didn't believe made it difficult for Paul and for those Gentiles who had believed and were saved. Paul wrote to the Thessalonians telling them that the Jews who opposed the Gentiles were heaping up "their sins to the limit" (1 Thessalonians 2:16). How long could this go on for?

The full number of Gentiles

In Romans 11:25 we read:

> I do not want you to be ignorant of this mystery, brothers, so that you may not be conceited: Israel has experienced a hardening in part until the full number of the Gentiles has come in.

What does this mean? Well, it could mean one of two things.

It could mean that when the right number of wild olive branches had been grafted in, the old olive tree would bloom and blossom and bear abundant fruit. That is, when the full number of Gentiles had been brought in Israel would repent and accept Jesus as the Christ (Messiah). He would then return and the times of refreshing would come in and the kingdom would be restored to Israel. And that was the desired result.

However, it could mean that when sufficient wild branches had been grafted in, the olive tree was not provoked into greater blossom and better fruit, and so it was cut down. Which was it to be? All Israel saved or the olive tree of Israel cut down?

Isaiah 6

If we read through Acts we find opposition from many within Israel, and especially from the leadership, and this continued right to the end of Acts. About the time Paul reached Rome in Acts 28, Josephus wrote the following:

> The high priest, Ananus the Younger, a Sadducee .... Assembled the Sanhedrin of the judges and brought before them the brother of Jesus, who was called Christ, whose name was James and some others; and when he had formed an accusation against them as breakers of the law, he delivered them to be stoned. (Josephus: *Antiquities of the Jews*: 20,19,1)

And one tradition has it that John and all the Christian leadership in Jerusalem were stoned along with James.

Meanwhile, in Rome, Paul preached Christ to the Jewish leaders and some believed and some did not (Acts 28:24). By this time the hardness of heart of Israel made them unable to hear the words of the Apostles or see the significance of the miraculous signs they did, and so Paul quoted at them the very judgmental words of Israel 6:9-10; see Acts 28:25-27. But the judgment of Isaiah 6 is that of *cutting down trees*. We read of the terebinth and oak being cut down in Isaiah 6:13. And so it was that the olive tree of Israel was cut down at Acts 28:25-27 and the very next verse tells us that "God's salvation has been sent to the Gentiles" (Acts 28:28).

No longer were Gentiles being saved to provoke Israel; that was all over. No longer were Gentile converts being grafted into the olive tree of Israel; there was no longer any tree for them to be grafted into. It had been cut down. And that is still the situation today. Christians in this age of grace are members of the Body of Christ, not joined-on members of Israel. Israel's hope is for a kingdom upon this earth; our hope is to be blessed in the heavenly places in Christ (Ephesians 1:3; 2:6-8). Two very different situations.

Part 5

Comments and Queries about Paul's Later Letters

28 Prayer is a weapon
True or false?

There is no doubt about it! Prayer is very important, essential, in fact. However, is prayer a weapon against the devil?

The prayers of Ephesians

If we look at the prayers in Ephesians we can see just how essential prayer is. Paul opened with a prayer of thanks for the faith and love of the Ephesians (1:15-19). He then prayed that God may give them wisdom and revelation to know Him better. And then he requested that that the eyes of their heart would be enlightened in order that they may know:

1.   The hope to which He has called you;
2.   The riches of His glorious inheritance;
3.   His incomparably great power.

There is, however, nothing here to suggest that prayer is a weapon.

The second prayer in Ephesians 3:16-19 is another magnificent prayer, asking first that the Ephesians may be strengthened by the power of the Spirit so that Christ may dwell in their hearts by faith. This is followed up with a request that they may be rooted and established in love, and that power may enable them to grasp how wide and long and high and deep is the love of Christ so that they may be filled to the measure of the fullness of God. That is an amazing prayer, but are there any words in it which would lead us to think that prayer is an offensive weapon against the powers of evil?

In concluding his letter Paul instructed them to "pray in the Spirit on all occasions with all kinds of prayers and requests. With this in mind, be alert and always keep on praying for all the saints" (Ephesians 6:18). Finally, Paul requests that they pray for him so that he will 'fearlessly' make known the mystery of the gospel. And he asks this twice (verses 19 & 20). These concluding verses show just how important Paul thought prayer was, but is there anything about prayer being a spear, or any other weapon, to ward off Satan?

The armour of God

We are told in Ephesians 6:12 that our struggle is not against flesh and blood. Rather it is:

- against the rulers and authorities of this dark world and
- against the spiritual forces of evil in the heavenly realms.

How are we to combat these?

First, it does not tell us to 'attack' them. Rather it tells us to put on the full armour of God and 'defend' our position. Three times, in Ephesians 6:13-14, we are told to 'stand'.

> Therefore put on the full armour of God, so that when the day of evil comes, you may be able to *stand* your ground, and after you have done everything to *stand*. *Stand* firm then …

We then have a description of what makes up this armour. There are six pieces. Is prayer a part of it?

The Armor of God

1. The belt of truth.
2. The breastplate of righteousness.
3. Sandals of the gospel of peace.
4. Shield of faith.
5. Helmet of salvation.
6. The sword of the Spirit, which is the word of God.

So we can see that prayer is not listed as part of the armour and there seems no place in the Scriptures where it is depicted as an offensive weapon. On the other hand, today there are books with titles such as *Prayer Warfare* and *Spiritual Warfare Prayer*.

> Prayer is the Christian's secret weapon and is like an intercontinental ballistic missile. They can be fired from any spot. They can travel undetected at the speed of light, hitting the target every time. Satan has no defence

There are illustrations of the armour of God with a soldier having not just a sword, but also a spear – the spear of prayer. And one can find posters which say 'Prayer; The believer's secret weapon,' but the only weapon believers have, according to the Ephesians 6, is "the sword of the spirit, which is the word of God."

Prayer and Study

I have had the privilege of speaking and visiting many different churches in a variety of denominations. In some of these churches I have heard such comments as, 'We would do much better if our people only prayed more!'

It seems over time various attendees have stopped coming; new people have come for a short while and then stopped. They have not been able to 'stand', for as soon as problems and difficulties arise, one of the first things to suffer is their faith and the remedy, according to some, seems to be prayer ... if only we had prayed more for these people. Again, I do not want to downplay the significance of such prayers, but is that diagnosis correct?

We are told in the Scriptures that:

> Faith comes from hearing the message, and the message is heard through the word of Christ. (Romans 10:17)

> The word of God is living and is active. Sharper than any double-edged sword, it penetrates even to dividing soul and spirit joints and marrow; it judges the thoughts and attitudes of the heart. (Hebrews 4:12)

So an increase of faith and understanding comes not from praying, but by hearing the word, from knowing what it says; as Timothy was told:

> How from infancy you have known the holy Scriptures, which are able to make you wise for salvation through faith in Christ Jesus. All Scripture is God-breathed and is useful for ...

> teaching,
> rebuking,
> correcting, and
> training in righteousness,
> so that the man of God may be
> thoroughly equipped for every good work.
> (2 Timothy 3:15-17).

If churches do not teach the Bible, if Christians do not know the Scriptures, they will not be 'thoroughly equipped'. And if the Christian soldier does not have "the sword of the Spirit, which is the word of God", he is not going to be thoroughly equipped for battle.

The sword of the Spirit

However, having a sword and being able to use it effectively are two different things. A young teenage girl living nearby took up sword fencing a year or so ago. If she challenged me to a duel, even though she is much smaller than I am, I doubt if I would last twenty seconds. I have seen a sword, I have held a sword, but I have never been trained and I have never practiced. I would be useless.

The expert swordsman was, of course, Christ Himself. When confronted by Satan in the wilderness He did not drop to His knees in prayer. Rather He answered each temptation with words from the Bible; see "it is written" in Matthew 4:4,6,10 and note the quotations from Deuteronomy 8:3; 6:16; 6:13.

Going back to some of those churches which say they are lacking in prayers ... I have observed in quite a few that no-one brings a Bible to church and there are no church Bibles in the pews, and although some may hold 'prayer meetings', few have 'Bible Studies'.

As the twentieth century progressed, in Britain Christian confidence in the authority of the Bible weakened – as noted by William Lane Craig in *Reasonable Faith*.

England is a much more secular country than the U.S. The most significant trend in British religious affiliation is the meteoric growth of those classed as "non-religious," who went from 0% of the population in 1900 to 34% today. British evangelical Christianity, we were told, tends to be charismatic and anti-intellectual, and many Christians are cowed into silence by the boisterous assertions of the New Atheists. According to *Operation World* were it not for the revitalizing impact of Christian immigrants to Britain, the English Church would be in a state of collapse. We saw evidence of the impact of immigrant Christians almost everywhere I spoke: many enthusiastic black and oriental faces greeted us after each event.

(William Lane Craig, *Reasonable Faith,* November 2011).

In some churches in Britain, Bible teaching has waned and Bible studies declined. As a result the full armour of God has not been put on. In some churches today there is almost an anti-intellectualism against Bible study.

Defence formation

In Ephesians 6 it seems Paul is describing a Roman division going into defence formation. When on the move they would march in a column, maybe four or six abreast. If they came under attack from arrows or stones or spears, they would go into defence formation. Romans had small round shields for hand to hand combat, but they also had the longer, rectangular shields which they marched with. When attacked *en route* those in the front put their shields in front of them. Those on the sides put their shields to the side, those in the middle, held their shields overhead. In this way they could ward off the 'flaming arrows' of the enemy.

However, they would also have their swords in their hands, and all Roman soldiers were skilled swordsmen. If they did not have their swords, or if they could not use them effectively, the rest of the armour would not be much use. The enemies could creep up close to them and spear them.

Prayer and study

So keep on praying, but also keep on studying or, if you haven't really started to study the Bible, please start doing so – and encourage others to do so also.

> Do your best to present yourself to God as one approved, a workman who does not need to be ashamed and who correctly handles the word of truth. (2 Timothy 2:15).

Are we soldiers who can correctly handle the sword of the Spirit, which is the word of God? If we are, we shall be approved of God. If we cannot, we may fall in the battle.

29 Christ dwells in every believer's heart True or false?

There is a common view that Jesus Christ dwells in the heart of every believer, but is that true? The idea was made popular by the hymn written by Emily Elliot which had the refrain:

> O come to my heart Lord Jesus,
> There is room in my heart for thee.

Was Miss Elliot correct in expressing that prayer, for a prayer it is? Is it possible for Christ, who according to Ephesians 1:20 sits at the right hand of God in the heavenly realms, to literally reside in our hearts?

Christ in you, the hope of glory

Surprisingly, perhaps, there is only one verse which has the expression "Christ in you", and that is Colossians 1:27.

> I have become its servant by the commission God gave me to present to you the word of God in its fullness — the mystery that has been kept hidden for ages and generations, but is now disclosed to the saints. To them God has chosen to make known among the Gentiles the glorious riches of this mystery, which is Christ in you, the hope of glory. (Colossians 1:25-27)

There are a number of things to note about this verse, and one of them is masked by modern translations. The *KJV* distinguished clearly between the second person singular (*ye*) and the second person plural (*you*). In the expression "Christ in you" it is the plural; "Christ in you". Thus this verse is not talking about an individual, it is referring to the saints (the common New Testament word for any believer), and to the Gentile saints in particular.

Also the Greek preposition *en* (translated 'in' here) when used with the plural is better translated 'among', and it has occurred earlier in this verse and there has been translated 'among'. That is:

To them God has chosen to make known among (*en*) the Gentiles the glorious riches of this mystery, which is Christ among (*en*) you (plural), the hope of glory.

Thus this verse is not talking about Christ dwelling **in** the hearts of believers, but about Christ dwelling *among* Gentile saints; in the midst of them, in the very centre. Is this significant? In its historical context, yes!

Christ among Israel

In the Old Testament, and through much of the New, the Jews were at the centre of God's plan. Gentiles could be blessed only through the seed of Abraham; i.e. Israel (Genesis 12:3). If Gentiles wanted direct access to God they needed to be circumcised (Exodus 12:48) and to keep the Sabbath Day (Isaiah 56:4-7), and so effectively become Jews.

This could be symbolised by the Tabernacle.

The Tabernacle In The Wilderness
Order of Camp: Levites Other Tribes

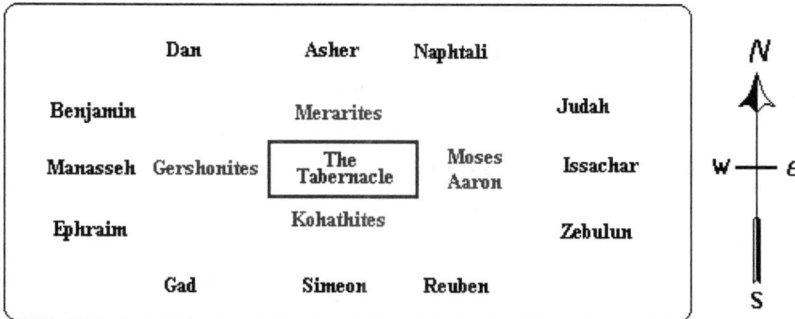

	Dan	Asher	Naphtali		N
Benjamin		Merarites		Judah	
Manasseh	Gershonites	The Tabernacle	Moses Aaron	Issachar	W — E
Ephraim		Kohathites		Zebulun	
	Gad	Simeon	Reuben		S

Daily Bible Study

God's glory dwelt in the holy of holies in the tabernacle. This was surrounded by the priests and around them the Twelve Tribes. Any Gentile wanting access to God had to go through Israel. God was indeed swelling 'among' Israel, in the midst of them. He was in the centre of Israel.

Even in the New Testament Israel continued to have first place and great advantages, even during the Acts period. Romans was the last letter Paul wrote during the Acts period and there we read that Israel had to have the gospel first; they had the blessings (and judgements) first, and they had the advantage (Romans 1:16; 2:9-10; 3:1-2). Also those early Gentile converts were seen as wild olives grafted into the cultivated olive tree of Israel and were fed by the nourishing sap from Israel's root (Romans 11:17).

However, Israel not only rejected their Messiah, they continually opposed the Apostles for the next thirty or so years, arguing against them, imprisoning them, beating them, killing them. At the end of Acts, following the final pronouncement of Isaiah's judgmental prophecy upon Israel (Acts 28:26-27), we read:

> God's salvation has been sent to the Gentiles, and they will listen. (Acts 28:28)

What is different here? In Old Testament times Gentiles could be saved, but they had to go through Israel. During the Acts period Gentiles were being saved, but the missionary work was being carried out by Jews and so the Gentiles were still being blessed through Israel. Here, at the end of Acts, the difference is that God's salvation was to be sent to the Gentiles independently of Israel and so, from then on, Christ was 'among' the Gentiles and, in this, God was doing something new.

This is what Colossians 1:25-27 is dealing with. Here Paul wrote about a mystery – the word means 'secret'. God revealed something secret which had been hidden for ages and generations. It was revealed at that time, at the end of Acts, to the saints. To the believers at that time God chose to make known that Christ was now centred among the Gentiles; He was no longer in the centre of Israel; He was in the centre of the Gentile Church, the Body of Christ.

But what about Christ dwelling in our hearts?

Is it possible for Christ to dwell in our hearts? After all, we are told that at present He is "seated at the right hand of God in the heavenly realms" (Ephesians 1:20). The answer is nowhere in Scripture does it talk about Christ *literally* dwelling in the hearts of believers. Some people think that it does, but that is a misunderstanding of Paul's second prayer in Ephesians. There we read:

> I pray that out of his glorious riches he may strengthen you with power through his Spirit in your inner being, so that Christ may dwell in your hearts *through faith*. (Ephesians 3:16-17a)

As Christ is now seated in the heavenly realms, how can He also be in the hearts of believers? This is, indeed, a problem.

However, note here that the prayer is that "Christ may dwell in your hearts *through faith*". That seems to imply it is not a 'literal' dwelling of Christ, who is now seated in the heavenly realms, but one in which the believer 'reckons' on Christ dwelling in his heart.

The word for 'dwell' means 'feel at home'. To have Christ feeling at home in the heart is not something that happens to people as soon as they believe. Paul was praying this for people who had been believers for years and later, in Ephesians 4:30, Paul makes it clear that believers can "grieve the Holy Spirit of God with whom you are sealed for the day of redemption". Verses 29 and 31 list some of the actions and attitudes that can grieve the Spirit. However, if we are causing the Spirit to grieve, then we can be sure that Christ most certainly does not feel at home in our heart.

What happens when we believe?

Many people seem to think that when we believe the gospel of salvation Christ immediately comes and lives in our hearts and then, sometime later, we can receive the Holy Spirit. Such a view is based upon misapplication and misunderstanding.

The misapplication comes from misunderstanding the Acts period. It is true that during that time *Jewish* Christians did not always receive the Holy Spirit when they first believed (e.g. Acts 19:1-6). However, the *Gentile* Christians did (e.g. Cornelius and company; Acts 10:43-44). That was the situation during Acts. However, after Acts Ephesians makes it clear that now all receive the Spirit when they believe the gospel of salvation:

> And you also were included in Christ when you heard the word of truth, the gospel of your salvation. Having believed, you were marked in him with a seal, the promised Holy Spirit. (Ephesians 1:13)

Thus Christ, *through His Spirit*, lives in us from the moment we believe, but does He immediately feel at home? That is the issue.

The second prayer of Ephesians tells us that if we want Christ to feel at home in our hearts through faith, we need to be more than nominal Christians. We need to be strengthened with power through His Spirit in our inner beings (Ephesians 3:16).

> The experience of the indwelling Spirit and the indwelling Christ is the same experience.
>
> F F Bruce; p 326, *The New International Commentary on the New Testament*

> I pray that out of his glorious riches he may strengthen you with power through his Spirit in your inner being, so that Christ may dwell in your hearts through faith.
> And I pray that you, being rooted and established in love, may have power, together with all the saints, to grasp how wide and long and high and deep is the love of Christ, and to know this love that surpasses knowledge—that you may be filled to the measure of all the fullness of God. (Ephesians 3:16-19)

In this two part prayer, the climax of the first is that "Christ may dwell in your hearts by faith". The climax of the second is "that you may be filled to the measure of the fullness of God".

The first is gained by being strengthened "with power through His Spirit in your inner being". The second is by knowing "this love that surpasses knowledge". We are filled with all the fullness of God when we not only know and appreciate God's love for us, but when we also acknowledge His love by putting it into practice and loving others as He loves us. When we do that, then Christ can feel at home in our hearts.

30 Women should not teach men
True or false?

When writing to Timothy Paul gave many instructions concerning prayer, men and women, overseers, and deacons. Much of it is non-controversial, but one passage has been the source of much debate in Christian circles: that is 1 Timothy 2:11-14.

> A woman should learn in quietness and full submission. I do not permit a woman to teach or to have authority over a man; she must be silent. For Adam was formed first, then Eve. And Adam was not the one deceived; it was the woman who was deceived and became a sinner.

Men, women and prayer

Earlier in this chapter, Paul had written:

> I want men everywhere to lift up holy hands in prayer, without anger or disputing. (1 Timothy 2:8)

Because of this verse some do not allow women to pray in church, insisting that here the Bible teaches that only men should pray. However, if we look at 1 Corinthians 11:5 we read about women who prayed in the church at Corinth and, if it was permitted in Corinth, then no doubt it was permitted elsewhere.

It is more likely that the emphasis in 1 Timothy 2:8 is on the *manner* in which *men* ought to pray, telling them they should not pray in meetings if they were angry and had just been in an argument, possibly disputing and debating doctrinal issues.

Women teaching

When we read of 'prophecy' our immediate thoughts turn to the future. However, a prophet was someone who spoke about God, saying what God did in the past, what He is doing in the present, or what He will do in the future. Thus a prophet, although not the same as, was not dissimilar to a teacher. In the same passage we noted earlier, 1 Corinthians 11:5, we read of women prophesying, and Philip had four daughters who were prophetesses (Acts 21:9).

We also read of Priscilla and Aquila teaching Apollos, and *they* "explained to him the way of God more adequately," (Acts18:24-26). It would appear, then, that Priscilla did some of the teaching, as well as Aquila. Paul described them as "my fellow-workers in Christ Jesus" in Romans 16:3, and we learn that there was a church in their home (1 Corinthians 16:19).

At the end of Romans we read of two of Paul's relatives, Andronicus and Junias who had been in prison with Paul and who were "outstanding among the apostles" (Romans 16:7). Like Paul (whose original name was Saul) they had Greek names which may mean that they, too, were from Tarsus. However, *The Companion Bible* note on Junias is ambiguous, stating that the word is in the accusative case and it may indicate 'Junias' (masculine) or 'Junia' (feminine). Strong, in his *Exhaustive Concordance*, indicates that it is 'Junia' and some ancient manuscripts have 'Julia'. If that is the case then we have a female apostle, and apostles did both prophesy and teach.

From the Old Testament it is clear that Israel's leaders were men, with the notable exception of Deborah. It is also true that the majority of prophets were men, but again there were a number of exceptions. The following women were prophetesses: Miriam (Exodus 15:20); Deborah (Judges 4:4); Huldah (2 Kings 22:14; 2 Chronicles 34:22-28). In the New Testament Anna is called a prophetess (Luke 2:36). However, it is clear from the New Testament that, with few exceptions, the teachers and prophets were mainly men.

But why didn't women teach?

In Old Testament times, and in the Judaism of the New Testament, Hebrew fathers had their sons educated in the Scriptures: the Law, the Prophets and the Psalms. They may have done some of this teaching themselves but, once the synagogue movement had been developed, the sons were also taught by the rabbi.

However, they did not teach their daughters because that was seen as the prerogative of the girl's future husband. There was great diversity in Judaism but it was essential that there should be unity in the home. It was, therefore, more important for a woman to agree with her husband's theology than her father's. Jewish women thus were basically uneducated, and so were in no way equipped to teach anyone.

On the other hand, Gentile women, especially those in the Greco-Roman world, could be highly educated, and this may have spread to some of the women of the Jewish dispersion. Priscilla was a Jewess from Rome (Acts 18:1-3) and was clearly a very able woman.

As we have mentioned, when we read through the New Testament we see just a few women in prominent positions, but we should also note that there were few, if any, Gentile men in prominent positions. Why was that?

> What advantage, then, is there in being a Jew, or what value is there in circumcision? Much in every way! First of all, the Jews have been entrusted with the very words of God. (Romans 3:1-2)

The Jewish Christians had an advantage (at that time) over the Gentile Christians: the Jewish Christians had the Scriptures and knew them; the Gentiles did not. It is not until well past the end of Acts that we see a Gentile, Titus, given a significant leadership role on the island of Crete, and that was some twenty years after he was saved (see Paul's letter to Titus).

Similarly, most of the women of that time (whether Jewish or Gentile) had little or no knowledge of the Scriptures. They were thus at a distinct disadvantage, needing to be taught, rather than to teach. However, as we have seen, there were exceptions. There may have been many more women prophets than there were women teachers. A prophet was inspired and enabled by the Holy Spirit to speak, but a teacher needed to know the Scriptures before he or she could explain them.

Women to be silent in the church

In 1 Corinthians 14:33-35 we have another controversial, and in some quarters misunderstood, passage. There we read:

> As in all the congregations of the saints, women should remain silent in the churches. They are not allowed to speak, but must be in submission, as the law says. If they want to inquire about something, they should ask their own husbands at home; for it is disgraceful for a woman to speak in the church.

This passage has been used to support the idea that women should not preach, pray or say anything in the church. However, such a view is clearly incorrect for we have already read, in 1 Corinthians 11:5, that women prayed and prophesied in the Corinthian church.

Some suggest that 1 Corinthians 14 is dealing with women talking and chattering, but it is more likely that the women were discussing what was being taught, trying to understand it. Here they are told, and again this is in harmony with what we have said earlier, to ask their own husbands at home.

Woman = wife; man = husband

However, there is another problem with 1 Timothy 2:11-14. Because the Greek word for 'woman' (*gune*) is also the Greek word for 'wife', and is translated so in many places (e.g. Acts 5:1,2,7; 18:2; 24:24; Ephesians 5:23,33). Also the Greek word for 'man' (*aner*) is translated 'husband' in the majority of places (e.g. Acts 5:9,10; Ephesians 5:23,33). Thus this passage could, and probably should, be translated:

> A *wife* should learn in quietness and full submission. I do not permit a *wife* to teach or to assume authority over a *husband*. (See footnotes in the *New Revised Standard Version* and in the

2010 edition of the *New International Version* and notes on 1
Timothy 2:9 in *The Companion Bible*.)

This translation, and its consequent interpretation, is in harmony with
what we wrote earlier about the non-education of Jewish daughters and
the desire for homes to be a unity and the need for a woman to be taught
by her own husband so as to preserve domestic unity. It is also in
harmony with what we read elsewhere in Scripture; for example in 1
Peter 3:1-2:

> Wives, in the same way be submissive to your husbands so that,
> if any of them do not believe the word, they may be won over
> without words by the behaviour of their wives, when they see the
> purity and reverence of your lives.

Peter wrote to the Jewish dispersion scattered over various parts of the
world (1 Peter 1:1). Some, in those synagogues, had become Christians;
but what if a woman came to believe Jesus to be the Christ, the Messiah,
her Saviour, but her husband did not? She was *not* to 'teach' him. She
was to leave that to the Christian men in the community.

Eve deceived

There are those who advocate that women should not teach men because
women are more easily deceived than men. They are more likely to
misunderstand God's Word and so teach error and lead men astray. If
that be the case, why are women allowed to teach children and teenagers
in Sunday School? It would surely be far easier for the women to lead
youngsters astray than it would be to teach error to adult males who
knew their Scriptures.

It is much easier to deceive an uniformed person than one who is
knowledgeable. God gave His instructions to Adam and, one assumes,
Adam passed them on to Eve. Eve's knowledge may have been second-
hand and, as such, may have been a contributory factor as to why Satan
approached her and her vulnerability to his deception.

And it may well be true that many of the Christian women in New Testament times were easier to deceive than the men, but that was because they were less informed as they had not been so well taught in the Scriptures.

And what of women today? Are they easier than men to deceive in spiritual matters? That depends on how well they know and understand the Scriptures.

31 'All Scripture' refers to the Old Testament
True or false?

Some time ago I was in a meeting when someone said that he had just realised that when Paul wrote to Timothy and stated that "All Scripture is God-breathed and is useful for teaching, rebuking, correcting and training in righteousness", that Paul was referring only to the Old Testament. As such, this person felt he had ignored the Old Testament and was now avidly studying it.

In no way do I wish to deny that the Old Testament is God-breathed. Neither do I wish to demean it in any way, but I do query whether Paul meant only the Old Testament when he used the expression "**All** Scripture".

The Scriptures

In the four Gospels the words "The Scriptures" (plural) occur a number of times, and all clearly refer to our Old Testament in general. There are also numerous references to "The Scripture" (singular), which generally refer to some specific verse of the Old Testament, often a fulfilment of a prophecy: (a concordance of these words and other such h terms is given at the end of this chapter).

This is also the case with the Acts of the Apostles and it is generally the case with the letters, but there are some verses in them which seem to refer to something other than the Old Testament. Take for example 1 Corinthians 15:3-4. There we read:

> For what I received I passed on to you as of first importance: that Christ died for our sins *according to the Scriptures,* that he was buried, that he was raised on the third day *according to the Scriptures ...*

Where in the Old Testament do we read that Christ (the Messiah) was to die for our sins? The Suffering Servant passage of Isaiah 53 stops short of saying just that. And where in the Old Testament do we read that the Messiah was to die and be raised from the dead on the third day? If Paul was not alluding to the Old Testament, then to what was he referring?

Peter's view

In 1 Peter 2:6 Peter quotes from the Old Testament and refers to it as "Scripture", which is no surprise. Then in 2 Peter 1:20-21 we read:

> Above all, you must understand that no prophecy of Scripture came about by the prophet's own interpretation. For prophecy never had its origin in the will of man, but men spoke from God as they were carried along by the Holy Spirit.

Peter, writing to the dispersed Israelites (1 Peter 1:1; "elect, strangers in the world, scattered throughout …"), would hardly need to convince his readers of such a widely held view of the Old Testament Scripture. Could Peter have had something else in mind? Look at Peter's next usage of this word.

> Bear in mind that our Lord's patience means salvation, just as our dear brother Paul also wrote to you with the wisdom that God gave him. He writes the same way in all his letters, speaking in them of these matters. His letters contain some things that are hard to understand, which ignorant and unstable people distort, as they do *the other Scriptures,* to their own destruction. (2 Peter 3:15-16)

Here Peter implies that Paul's letters are Scripture! He says that some people distort Paul's letters, as they do "the *other* Scriptures". Which letters could Peter be referring to as Scripture? Almost certainly Galatians, which was probably Paul's first letter, as Peter sent his letters to those 'scattered throughout … Galatia' (1 Peter 1:1; 2 Peter 3:1). It is hard to date Peter's letters precisely, but 2 Peter was probably written towards the end of the Acts of the Apostles. By this time Paul would have written not only Galatians, but also 1 & 2 Thessalonians, 1 & 2 Corinthians and possibly Romans – leaving aside any discussion of Hebrews.

Also, was Peter referring to Old Testament prophecy in 2 Peter 1:20-21 or to some New Testament ones, like Revelation or 2 Thessalonians 2 or Matthew 24? These may well have been written and circulating by the time Peter wrote his second letter.

Paul's view

Thus we return to 1 Corinthians 15:3-4. What "Scriptures" did Paul have in mind when he wrote those words? Clearly it must have been one or more of the Gospels. It seems very likely that Mark was written quite soon after the Lord's ascension and John, too, may have been very early[24]. After all John's Gospel, more than any other, backed up what Paul was doing and teaching during the Acts of the Apostles.

At that time Paul was visiting Synagogues and addressing Jews, Proselytes and God-fearing Gentiles. His aim was to convince them that Jesus was the Christ (Messiah), the Son of God – e.g. Acts 9:20,22.

At once he began to preach in the synagogues that Jesus

The People

There are basically four groups of people in the New Testament

Jews – Descendants of Abraham through Isaac.
Proselytes – Gentiles who had adopted Judaism and who had been circumcised, and who are basically treated as Jews.
God-fearers – Gentiles who attended the synagogues but who had not become Proselytes.
Pagans – the rest of the Gentiles.

---

[24] See *The Priority of John* by John A T Robinson (SCM Press) and *Another Look at John's Gospel* by Ernest Streets (OBT). Also Appendix 2 of *Approaching the Bible* by Michael Penny (OBT) which deals with the dating of all John's writings. All favour an early date for John's Gospel.

is the *Son of God* ... Yet Saul grew more and more powerful and baffled the Jews living in Damascus by proving that Jesus is *the Christ (Messiah)*.

Now the very purpose of John's Gospel is just that:

> Jesus did many other miraculous signs in the presence of his disciples, which are not recorded in this book. But these are written that you may believe that Jesus is *the Christ (Messiah), the Son of God*, and that by believing you may have life in his name. (John 20:30-31)

John's Gospel is somewhat enigmatic. In some places it seems very Jewish, while in others it explains things which were obvious to Jews. However, if his target audience was the same as Paul's – a mixture of Jews, Proselytes and God-fearing Gentiles, one can understand why John wrote as he did.

Paul and Timothy

This brings us back to Paul's letters to Timothy. In 1 Timothy Paul quoted from the Old Testament and refers to it as "*The* Scripture" (5:18). Then, again, in his second letter we read:

> But as for you, continue in what you have learned and have become convinced of, because you know those from whom you learned it, and how from infancy you have known *the holy Scriptures*, which are able to make you wise for salvation through faith in Christ Jesus. (2 Timothy 3:14-15)

"The holy Scriptures" clearly refers to the Old Testament as when Timothy was an infant none of the New Testament documents had been written. However, to what is Paul referring in the next verse?

> *All Scripture* is God-breathed and is useful for teaching, rebuking, correcting and training in righteousness, so that the

man of God may be thoroughly equipped for every good work. (2 Timothy 3:16-17)

For Paul to tell Timothy that the Old Testament was God-breathed and useful for teaching, rebuking, and so on, would have been stating the obvious. However, if Paul had in mind certain New Testament documents then his statement becomes very understandable.

We know from the tenure of Paul's two letters to Timothy that Timothy, a wonderful servant of whom Paul could say "I have no one else like him" (Philippians 2:20), seems to have lost some of his enthusiasm. We know that the influence of Judaism was strong in Galatia (where Timothy came from) which was why Paul wrote the letter to the Galatians. Was Timothy slipping into a Judaistic way of life, based on the Law of Moses? If he was, then he would have become over-focused on the Old Testament (*The* Scriptures).

Without denigrating those Old Testament Scriptures in any way (see 2 Timothy 3:14-15), Paul seems to be reminding Timothy that **ALL** Scripture is God-breathed, including the new Scriptures, which became our New Testament. And he seems to be saying to Timothy that **ALL** Scripture, including the new Scriptures, is useful for teaching, rebuking, correcting and training in righteousness And that **ALL** Scripture, including the new Scriptures, is needed if the man of God is to become thoroughly equipped for every good work.

Today

Returning to the comments of the friend mentioned in the opening paragraph: in general I find many Christians spend more time reading the Old Testament than they do the letters, and that they have a better understanding of the Old Testament than they do of the epistles of the New Testament. If that is the case, then Paul's words to Timothy should be heeded.

All Scripture, including Paul's letters (as Peter includes them in the Scriptures), is needed if we are to become thoroughly equipped for every good work. After all, Paul is the only person called 'The Apostle to the Gentiles' and we are Gentiles (Romans 11:13; Galatians 2:8). Thus we ignore his letters to our peril. It may be better to spend more time on Ephesians than on either Exodus or Ezekiel!

Concordance of 'Scripture'

Readers may wish to look up each of the following references, some of which are alluded to or quoted in this article. (This is not a full list of all of the occurrences.)

The Scriptures
Matthew 21:42; 22:29; 26:54
Mark 12:24; 14:49;
Luke 24:27,32,45
John 5:39 (twice)
Acts 17:2,11; 18:24,28
Romans 15:4
1 Corinthians 15:3,4

The Holy Scriptures
Romans 1:2
2 Timothy 3:15

Scripture
Luke 4:21
John 19:37
Acts 8:35
James 4:5,6
1 Peter 2:6
2 Peter 1:20

The Scripture
John 2:22; 7:38,42; 10:35; 17:12; 19:24,28,36; 20:9
Acts 1:16
Romans 4:3; 9:17; 10:11; 11:2
Galatians 3:8,16,22; 4:30
1 Timothy 5:18
James 2:23

The Other Scriptures
2 Peter 3:16

All Scripture
2 Timothy 3:16

Publications Quoted and Referred to

Allen, Olive and Lloyd: *The Church! When did it begin? (And why is that important?)*

Anthony, Metropolitan: *Jesus: Then and Now*

Babylonian Talmud

Barker, Jason Jay: *Be Transformed: An Interactive Study of the Epistle to the Romans*

Bauer, Walter: *A Greek-English Lexicon of the New Testament and Other Early Christian Literature*

Blaiklock, E M; *Tyndale New Testament Commentary*

Bruce, F F: *New International Commentary on the New Testament*

Bullinger, E W: *The Companion Bible*

Burch, Helaine: *Asleep in Christ*

Comfort, Philip W: *The Origin of the Bible*

Craig, William Lane: *Reasonable Faith*

Creed, J M: *The Gospel According to St. Luke*

Eusebius: *Ecclesiastical History*

Evans, Mary: *Woman in the Bible*

Geldenhuys, Norval: *Commentary on the Gospel of Luke*

Josephus, Flavius: *The Antiquities of the Jews*

Mackintosh, C H: *Notes on the Pentateuch*

Manson, T W: *The Mission and Message of Jesus*

Martin, Ralph P: *Philippians: An Introduction and Commentary*

Meinardus, Otto F A: *Two Thousand Years of Coptic Christianity*
Midrash

Morgan, D Campbell: *The Acts of the Apostles*

Moule, C F D: *Expository Times* (Article)

Murcot, Peter: *British Church Newspaper* (Article)

New Bible Dictionary

Ozanne, Charles: *The Life & Soul of Mortal Man*

Penny, Michael: *40 Problem Passages*
 Approaching The Bible
 A Systematic Approach to Parables (CDs)
 Deuteronomy 28: A key to understanding
 The Miracles of the Apostles
 The New Covenant. Who is it with? When is it for?

The Place of Prayer in an Age of Grace
The Purpose of the Parables
True or False? Questions and Queries about Christianity
Penny, Sylvia: *Woman to Woman*
Robinson, J A T: *The Priority of John*
Stephens, Neville: *Unanswered Prayer*
Streets, Ernest: *Another Look At the Gospel of John*
Think On These Things
Strong, James: *Exhaustive Concordance of the Bible*
Vine, W E: *Expository Dictions of New Testament Words*
Wickes, Roland: *The Path to Immortality*
Williams, Don: *The Apostle Paul and Women in the Church*
Williams, George: *The Student's Commentary*
Young, Robert: *Literal Translation of the Bible*

Translations of the Bible used

The main quotations are taken from the *New International Version*.
Others include:

Amplified
ASV
ESV
GNB
Interlinear Greek-English New Testament
KJV
LXX
Moffatt
NASV
NKJV
NRSV
REB
Young's Literal Translation

Further Reading

True or False?

Comments and Queries about
Christianity
by Michael Penny

Are these True or False?

- This is the best of all possible worlds.
- Christians should practise what they preach.
- Heaven is perfect.
- The Kingdom is extended by kindness
- Sexual morals are out of date.
- It is impossible to know God.
- Suffering shows there is no God.
- God calls us home.
- We should do what Jesus would do.
- Christ condoned adultery.
- The Holy Spirit can be taken from us.

These and twenty other comments and queries are discussed in a thought provoking manner. The aim of the author is to encourage people to 'think' about what they hear and read, and about what they believe. Which of the above are true? Which are false?

Available from **www.obt.org.uk** and from

The Open Bible Trust,
Fordland Mount, Upper Basildon,
Reading, RG8 8LU, UK.

Also available as an eBook.

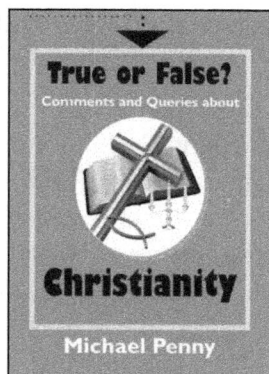

About the author

Michael Penny was born in Ebbw Vale, Gwent, Wales in 1943. He read Mathematics at the University of Reading, before teaching for twelve years and becoming the Director of Mathematics and Business Studies at Queen Mary's College Basingstoke in Hampshire, England. In 1978 he entered Christian publishing, and in 1984 became the administrator of The Open Bible Trust.

He held this position for seven years, before moving to the USA and becoming pastor of Grace Church in New Berlin, Wisconsin. He returned to Britain in 1999, and is at present the Administrator and Editor of The Open Bible Trust. From 2010 he has been Chairman of Churches Together in Reading, where he speaks in a number of churches of different denominations. He is also a member of the Advisory Committee to Reading University Christian Union and a chaplain at Reading College. He lives near Reading with his wife and has appeared on Premier Radio and BBC Radio Berkshire many times. He has made several speaking tours of America, Canada, Australia, New Zealand and the Netherlands, as well as others to South Africa and the Philippines. Some of his writings have been translated into German and Russian.

He has written many books including *Paul: A Missionary of Genius, Peter: His Life and letters, James: His life and letter; 40 Problem Passages, Galatians: Interpretation and Application, Joel's Prophecy: Past and Future, Approaching the Bible* plus two written with William Henry: *The Will of God: Past and Present* and *Following Philippians*.

Further details of these, and other publications, can be seen on

www.obt.org.uk/michael-penny

The above are available as both perfect bound books (from the Open Bible Trust) and eBooks (from Amazon Kindle and Apple iBooks).

www.ingramcontent.com/pod-product-compliance
Lightning Source LLC
Chambersburg PA
CBHW071531040426
42452CB00008B/976